you know you're in
arizona when ...

979.1 L951
Lowe, Sam.
You know you're in Arizona
  when

MID-CONTINENT PUBLIC LIBRARY
Boardwalk Branch
8656 N. Ambassador Dr. **BW**
Kansas City, MO 64154

WITHDRAWN
FROM THE RECORDS OF THE
MID-CONTINENT PUBLIC LIBRARY

D1301936

Some Other Books in the Series

You Know You're In Series

you know you're in
arizona when...

101 Quintessential Places, People, Events, Customs, Lingo, and Eats of the Grand Canyon State

Sam Lowe

INSIDERS' GUIDE®

GUILFORD, CONNECTICUT
AN IMPRINT OF THE GLOBE PEQUOT PRESS

MID-CONTINENT PUBLIC LIBRARY
Boardwalk Branch
8656 N. Ambassador Dr.
Kansas City, MO 64154 **BW**

MID-CONTINENT PUBLIC LIBRARY

3 0000 12631473 5

To buy books in quantity for corporate use
or incentives, call **(800) 962–0973, ext. 4551,**
or e-mail **premiums@GlobePequot.com.**

INSIDERS' GUIDE®

Copyright © 2005 by The Globe Pequot Press

All rights reserved. No part of this book may be reproduced or transmitted in any form by any means, electronic or mechanical, including photocopying and recording, or by any information storage and retrieval system, except as may be expressly permitted by the 1976 Copyright Act or by the publisher. Requests for permission should be made in writing to The Globe Pequot Press, P.O. Box 480, Guilford, Connecticut 06437.

Insiders' Guide is a registered trademark of The Globe Pequot Press.

Text design and illustrations by Linda R. Loiewski

Library of Congress Cataloging-in-Publication Data
Lowe, Sam
    You know you're in Arizona when— : 101 quintessential places, people, events, customs, lingo, and eats of the Hrand Canyon State/Sam Lowe,—1st ed.
        p. cm.—(You know you're in series)
    Includes bibliographical references and index
    ISBN 0-7627-3816-2 (alk. paper)
    1. Arizona—Miscellanea. 2. Arizona—Description and travel—Miscellanea. I. Title. II. Series.
    F811.6.L69 2005
    979.1—dc22

                                    2005009295

Manufactured in the United States of America
First Edition/First Printing

To Arizona, whose charm and endless beauty
have sustainedand excited me for almost four decades.

about the author

Sam Lowe fled the Midwest and began his ongoing love affair with Arizona in 1969, shortly after he became accustomed to mowing his lawn in December. Over the ensuing years, he was a columnist for the *Phoenix Gazette* and *Arizona Republic* and has contributed hundreds of Arizona-oriented stories to a variety of national and international publications. He is also the author of *Arizona Curiosities,* published by The Globe Pequot Press; *If I Had An Elephant,* a compilation of his columns; and *Discover Arizona: The Desert,* published by Arizona Highways. He and his wife, Lyn, live in Phoenix.

to the reader

Writing about Arizona is easy. We have, after all, deserts and cacti, tall trees and dry rivers, mountains and sand dunes, rich historical lore and, in many cases, twisted logic that passes for politics. But boiling all that is Arizona into 101 things that are quintessential Arizona requires a delicate touch because there's always the possibility of omitting a thing of importance, or including something less than quintessential.

Fortunately for authors, the selection process is subjective. Everyone who attempts to compile lists such as this will find disagreement with those produced by anyone else. That's just how things are. And so, the items and stories in this book were chosen because in my mind, they are the shades and colors that make up the grandeur of Arizona.

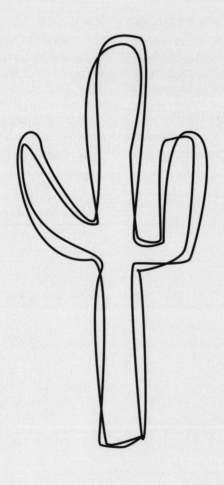

you know you're in
arizona when ...
... Apache tears tell a sad story

Just east of the small community of Superior, there's an escarpment known as Apache Leap. It plummets down toward the town before leveling out into a valley that is a favorite destination for rock hounds because of the abundance of Apache tears.

Geologically, Apache tears are obsidian, a dark-colored or black volcanic glass often used as a gemstone. They are the by-products of eruptions that occurred millions of years ago, and when they are removed from the ground they are usually covered with a white substance. Rock collectors like them because they polish easily.

But the legend of the Apache tears is much more interesting than their physical composition. According to stories handed down over the past century, in the 1870s a band of Apache warriors were trapped in the mountains by a U.S. cavalry unit. Unable to escape and not willing to surrender, the warriors hurled themselves to their deaths off the cliffs now called Apache Leap. Later, when their widows came to the scene, the women wept bitterly, and their tears turned to stone.

The portion of the legend about the warriors is true. The part about the tears turning to stone? Improbable. But then . . . .

Apache Tears:

Obsidian rocks with an interesting legend.

1

you know you're in
arizona when...
... you travel the Apache Trail

Among the few signs along the Apache Trail are a couple that indicate it's 43 miles from one end to the other. The signs don't describe the miles in any way. This can be deceptive to anyone not familiar with the roadway because, despite appearances on the map, the Apache Trail rarely goes straight. Instead it twists, turns, swivels, and writhes its way through the Superstition Mountains from Apache Junction to Roosevelt Dam.

A more helpful sign might say something like, "43 miles, some of them washboardy and interspersed with sharp curves and dropoffs so sheer they'll make your eyes pop out and your belly tighten up, so stay awake and don't look back because there might be some numbskull from out of state coming at you with a 40-foot mobile home."

Actually, the 43-mile stretch isn't all bad. It's paved from Apache Junction to Tortilla Flats, a small tourist attraction about halfway up. After that, however, it's so contorted it would give a rattlesnake a backache trying to maneuver it.

A one-lane bridge across Pine Creek is a momentary respite because the bridge is one of the few places where the road doesn't curve. This 50 yards or so of flat, uncomplicated roadway gives drivers a chance to exhale. But they need to do so quickly, because there's another turn just

Apache Trail:

Although only 43 miles long, it takes almost four hours to drive it from one end to the other because it twists, turns, rises, falls, and plummets into the Superstition Mountains.

ahead and more after that. Each must be given a driver's full attention because every glance downward or to the side conjures up demons who plant thoughts about how dead you'd be if you plunged into a canyon. So the signs that urge speeds of ten miles per hour deserve and demand respect.

And yet, there's also great beauty along the Trail. The canyon walls change hue as the sun moves across them, and the speedboats skittering across Canyon Lake resemble long-tailed bugs. But there's little chance to enjoy the sights: The Trail is only two lanes, and there are only a few places to pull over and stop.

Due to the perils involved, allow up to four hours to travel the Apache Trail.

... you pay a visit to Cochise and Geronimo

Cochise and Geronimo, two great Apache leaders, both lived part of their lives in Arizona.

Cochise, the principal leader of the Mimbreno Chiricahuas, led raids into Arizona from Mexico after he was falsely accused of kidnapping a white child in 1861. For more than ten years, he and his Apache warriors hid out in the Dragoon Mountains of southeastern Arizona. Eventually, he surrendered and was moved to New Mexico, where he died in 1874.

Geronimo, born in 1829 in what is now western New Mexico, became the most famous Apache leader of all time. His exploits began in 1858. Spanish soldiers killed five members of his family, and in retaliation he began terrorizing New Mexico, Old Mexico, and Arizona. During that time, he was nicknamed "Geronimo" (Spanish for Jerome) by Mexican soldiers.

When the federal government forced all Chiricahua Apaches onto the San Carlos Reservation in Arizona in 1876, Geronimo was among them, but he escaped several times. He finally surrendered to Gen. Nelson Miles in September 1886. But instead of returning him to San Carlos, the government shipped Geronimo to Florida, then to Fort Sill, Oklahoma, where he lived in captivity until his death in 1909.

Both warriors are minimally remembered in Arizona today. Cochise has a town and a county named after him in the southeastern corner of the state. Geronimo didn't fare quite as well. His namesake was once a small town along U.S. Highway 60, but today it's little more than a wide spot in the road. It's sort of fitting, in a way, because Geronimo's given name was Goyathlay, Apache for "one who yawns."

Apache Warriors:

Cochise and Geronimo both earned their reputations while living in Arizona.

you know you're in
arizona when...
...construction lasts for decades

The one thing most people recognize when they visit the city-of-the-future project named Arcosanti is that nobody seems to be in a hurry. Things are getting done, but at such a deliberate pace that those who frequently go there see very few changes.

The work started in 1970 and it's nowhere near finished. It's so far from completion, in fact, that the man who designed it probably won't be around to see it finished. Paolo Soleri, an Italian-born artist and architect, bought a large piece of high desert near Cordes Junction in the late 1960s and began work on what he hopes will be a self-supporting community of about 7,000 visionaries.

If it goes according to plan, all the residents will live in a single building that will also house the offices, stores, and other facilities necessary to operate a town. Solar power will generate energy; no motorized vehicles will be allowed in the community core; and the inhabitants will raise their own food on the surrounding acreage.

The buildings are, for the most part, half-spheres that face south to use the winter sun for heating while minimizing the heat of the summer sun. And, although progress is slow by modern standards, the work goes on at a steady pace. Some people have already moved in as permanent residents, and concerts are staged regularly in a new music center.

Arcosanti is open for daily tours, and those who ask when it'll be done usually hear a variation of "When it gets done."

Arcosanti:

A futuristic urban complex that has been under construction in the Arizona desert for more than thirty years under the guidance of architect Paolo Soleri.

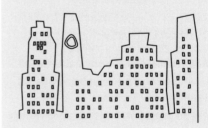

you know you're in
arizona when...
...the name escapes you

Eventually, if you're one of the state's 5.74 million (and growing rapidly) residents, somebody's going to ask you where the name Arizona came from. The answers are many, ranging from old Spanish terms to a babbling brook to "Anozira spelled backwards."

But the truth is: Nobody knows for certain.

The most popular theory is that it evolved from ali and shonak, two words from the Tohono O'odham tribal dialect that, when used together, mean "small springs." Many believe that early Spanish explorers and settlers found that name hard to pronounce and changed it to Arissona, which was eventually changed to Arizona by cowboys who found that even easier to pronounce.

Others say the name comes from a Basque phrase meaning "the good oak tree." Basque sheepherders applied it to an area in the southern portion of what is now Arizona, where the trees were once plentiful.

Arizona:

Where'd they get that name? Its origins are still in question.

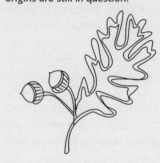

you know you're in
arizona when . . .
. . . Rangers aren't just in parks

The Arizona Rangers were formed in 1901 to combat the cattle rustlers who roamed and pillaged southeastern Arizona along the Mexican border. As undercover agents, they disguised themselves as cowboys and ranch hands so they could infiltrate the rustling operations. Once they got the goods on their suspects, they produced their badges and made the arrests.

But the Rangers had a change of assignment when copper miners went on strike. After the state legislature enacted a law that shortened the miners' working day without cutting their pay, the mine owners responded by reducing both the work shifts and the paychecks. Upset by the treachery, the miners armed themselves and took to the streets.

The Rangers, allied with the mine owners, were ordered to Morenci for what could have been a major showdown. But in the end, the weather settled the issue. The summer monsoons came early and flooded the community, and miners elected to save their families and possessions rather than fight.

Arizona Rangers:

A small army of lawmen who helped tame the wild West.

Although they were successful and would eventually be immortalized in literature and films, the Rangers lasted only eight years. They were given the boot in 1909, primarily because areas not affected by rustling and strikes didn't want to pay the taxes required to pay their salaries.

A television series called *26 Men* gave the Rangers another moment in the spotlight in the 1970s.

you know you're in
arizona when...
... you throw an atlatl

Each month, the Phoenix chapter of the Study of Aboriginal Lifeways and Technologies (SALT) holds meetings to show prospective big-game hunters how to use an atlatl (pronounced just like it's spelled—at-LAT-l). This acient device preceded the bow and arrow as a weapon.

The atlatl itself is a piece of wood, bone, or antler about 24 inches long with a curved, hooklike protrusion on one end. Darts measuring between 5 and 7 feet long are fitted into the hook and lie on top of the atlatl. The user (probably called an *atlatlist* even though it's hard to pronounce) grips the atlatl, cocks his hand back, and, while holding the dart down with one finger, hurls it forward in a motion similar to that of a pitcher throwing a baseball. But, unlike a baseball pitcher, the hunter hangs onto the atlatl while the spear goes hurtling toward its target.

For obvious reasons, the atlatl is not a common sight at deer-hunter conventions. But those interested can look at one in any of several museums around the state. If you decide that's what you want to use to bring down your next moose, you can attend a SALT meeting. For more information, go to www.worldatlatl.org or www.world atlatl.biz.

Atlatl:

A hunting weapon used long before the bow and arrow, now making a comeback.

Thirty-five miles east of Flagstaff, along Interstate 40, there's this big hole in the ground where the sky fell in. It's almost a mile in diameter and at one point was almost 1,500 feet deep.

Although the object that created it measured only about 100 feet across, there are, of course, some extenuating circumstances. The thing was from outer space. It weighed more than 50,000 tons. And it was traveling at an estimated 43,000 miles an hour when it hit the ground.

The meteorite collided with Earth about 49,500 years ago. The hole it made, now called Meteor Crater, draws more than 300,000 tourists every year. Even folks from NASA have been known to hang around there.

Much larger meteorites have plunged into Earth's surface, but Meteor Crater is the best preserved. By the time early white explorers found it around 1870, it was only about 600 feet deep, but test drillings in the early 1900s hit meteorite fragments at 1,000 feet and a large chunk of outer space rock at 1,376 feet.

Big Hole (extraterrestrial):

Meteor Crater was created when an object from outer space smacked into Earth nearly 50,000 years ago.

Philadelphia mining engineer D. Moreau Barringer bought the crater in 1902 and dug around in it until his funds ran out in 1929. The site is still owned by the Barringer family, which opened a new multi-million-dollar visitor center in 2002. Tourists are not allowed to climb down into the crater, but people wearing space suits get special permission. All the Apollo astronauts underwent extensive training here before leaving for the moon.

arizona when ...

... big holes are dug by big boys with really big toys

Things from outer space can make some major dents on the planet, but Earthlings are no slouches either when it comes to creating big holes. You need only look at Arizona's copper mining industry to understand how big a hole a person can dig when the right tools are available.

The Morenci Mine is a prime example. A large area now filled with nothing, it used to hold billions of tons of dirt and rock. The open pit mine, owned and operated by Phelps Dodge, is 2,500 feet deep and 2 miles across, with a 9-mile perimeter. That means two Meteor Craters could fit inside and there'd still be plenty of room left for tour-bus parking and gift shops.

The toys that dig holes like this are also big. Very big. The scoop shovel is so tall that the operator has to take an elevator up to the controls. The trucks that haul about 800,000 tons of ore every day are 20 feet tall, have a wheelbase of 20 feet, and can hold 1,000 gallons of fuel.

A few miles south in Bisbee, another pit just sits there and gapes. After producing copper ore for twenty-three years, the Lavendar Pit was shut down in 1974. Before it closed, miners extracted 375 million tons of stuff from the ground, leaving a hole that measures 1,000 feet deep, three-quarters of a mile wide, and 1.5 miles long, and covers 600 acres.

There's a chain-link fence surrounding it so gawkers don't fall in.

Big Holes (industrial):

Humans are no slouches when it comes to making dents in the Earth's surface.

you know you're in
arizona when ...
... you wear a dead scorpion around your neck

This should probably be listed under the "good news, bad news" section.

The good news: Arizona is the only state in the union where the state legislature has designated official neckwear.

The bad news: The neckwear is the bola tie.

The bola is loved by many, scorned by many. It consists of a leather thong and a sliding clasp that adjusts the tie to the wearer's neck without going through the hassle of tying a knot. The clasp is the focal point. Some clasps are splendid creations, almost works of art. They're made of silver, gold, turquoise, petrified wood, gemstones, hardwoods, carved animal horn, and ceramics.

Other clasps can be, well, a bit tacky. Among the hottest sellers in tourist-oriented gift shops are bola ties with clasps featuring scorpions encased in plastic. Or coyote droppings encased in plastic. Or elk droppings varnished to a satin sheen. Or even hula girls that wiggle when the wearer nods his head.

The bola was invented in the 1940s by Arizona cowboy Vic Cedarstaff of Wickenburg, who hung a fancy hatband around his neck. When a friend complimented him on his choice of neckwear, Cedarstaff made some improvements and the bola took on a life of its own.

It was proclaimed the state's official neckwear in 1971. However, wearing a bola tie is not mandatory for either living in or conducting business in Arizona.

Bola Tie:

The official neckwear of Arizona.

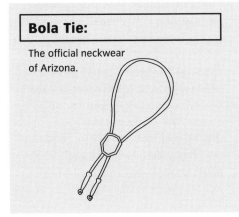

...not all boots are made for walking

Some birds like saguaro cacti because they can be easily converted into high-rise, single-family residences. And because they keep them safe from predators, particularly snakes and other critters that would rather go hungry than shinny up a fully spined cactus.

The birds—usually wrens, woodpeckers, and flickers—drill into the exterior of a saguaro and hollow out a nest inside. The excavations don't hurt the plant because it has an ingenious way of stopping leaks. Its spongy, pithy inner cells are tiny water bags with thin walls that water seeps through, and the outer cells contain a sticky, mucilage-like substance. When the outside shell is punctured and air touches the mucilage, the "glue" hardens and coats the inside of the hole, stopping the leak and preventing loss of moisture.

The saclike pouches are called "boots," and they outlast the cactus itself. When the initial residents move on, the insulated holes serve as quarters for a variety of

Boots:

The birds that make their nests by drilling into a saguaro cactus also produce this byproduct that can be used by an artist.

owls. In the old days, when the cactus eventually died, the Indians removed the boot and used it as a water bottle or a storage unit like today's plastic containers. But today, artists convert many of the boots into brightly decorated art objects to sell in the gift shops at botanical gardens and museums.

you know you're in
arizona when ...
... bridges don't always go across water

Arizona is big on bridges. Or, make that Arizona has some big bridges. Two of them are the world's largest in their respective categories, which is notable because neither of them spans a large body of water.

The Tonto Natural Bridge, northeast of Payson, is the world's largest travertine bridge. The natural marble span stands 183 feet high over a 400-foot-long tunnel that measures 150 feet at its widest point. According to geologists and engineers, construction started more than two billion years ago when the western edge was formed by a lava flow. The lava eroded and the remaining rock layers were tilted, faulted, flooded, tossed, turned, and eventually covered by more lava.

Then a mere 5,000 years ago, precipitation began seeping underground through fractures and weak points in the rock, resulting in limestone aquifers. Springs sprang from the aquifers, their water eroded the rock, and the bridge was formed. The travertine archway dwarfs those who go to stare at it and walk through it.

Tucson is home to the world's largest rattlesnake bridge. It's not made of rattlesnake hide, nor does it give rattlers access to the other side of the river. It's a pedestrian overpass designed to look like a snake.

The Diamondback Bridge, named after a species of rattlesnake, is 300 feet long, 16 feet high, and 16 feet across as it spans Broadway Road, a busy thoroughfare in downtown Tucson. After the project was authorized by the city, Tucson artist Simon Donovan was commissioned to convert steel floor grating into a rattlesnake. And he did, sort of. Pedestrians enter through simulated fangs at one end, and when they exit, an electronic eye triggers a rattling sound.

Modern-day Jonahs who wish to say they survived in the belly of a rattlesnake will find the bridge at First Avenue and Tenth Street as they cross Broadway Road.

Bridges:

Arizona has the world's largest travertine bridge and the world's largest rattlesnake bridge.

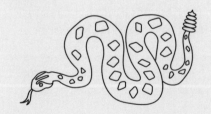

Burros are big in Oatman. They're protected, even coddled, because they're a primary source of income.

The burros are descendants of the pack animals used by early miners in their quests for gold more than a century ago. When they failed to find the mother lode and wound up broke and destitute, the old miners simply turned their beasts of burden loose in the surrounding hills.

Although apparently given a death sentence, the burros survived. And now, wise to the ways of humans, they have learned how to mine the tourists who flock to Oatman just to look at them. Every day shortly before noon, the animals come down from the hills and line up along Oatman's main drag, where they wait for handouts from the burro-watchers.

Local merchants have joined in the spirit by introducing merchandise that honors the creatures. They sell things like burro feed, burro figurines, burro T-shirts, burro bumper stickers, and burro calendars.

The animals have become such cash cows—uh, burros—that the townspeople

Burros:

Oatman has enacted special laws to protect the wild burros that make daily soirees into the community.

have enacted laws that protect the animals. Anyone who injures a burro is subject to a major fine. The community is also protecting the makings for its annual Burro Biscuit Toss, where contestants select solidified burro droppings and try to fling them farther than anyone else. Most of the tossers wash their hands afterwards. Those who don't, still get respect from the burros, as long as the hands hold a carrot.

you know you're in
arizona when...
...there's cactus everywhere

Cactus and Arizona make such a compatible couple. Even a casual mention of the state conjures up an image of a cowboy falling into a patch of prickly pear or a giant saguaro pointing its arms skyward in surrender to the desert.

This is probably because there are seventy-two species of cactus native to Arizona, the second most of any state in the union. (Texas is first, with eighty-five.) And, according to the cactus experts at the Boyce Thompson Arboretum in Superior, there may be as many as 1,800 nonnative species also growing in the state, either in the wild or in little pots on kitchen windowsills.

Cacti vary in size from the diminutive pincushion, usually the size of a shirt button, to the saguaro, which can grow to more than 50 feet. But they all have one thing in common: spines. Spines are a basic protection against being eaten by browsing animals.

Aside from several varieties of prickly pear, which seem to grow everywhere, cactus plants are quite selective about habitat. Most of the larger species—saguaro, organ pipe, barrel—reside in deserts well below the tree lines. But the paper-spined cactus grows only in clumps of gramma grass in a small area between Springerville and Show Low in the White Mountains. And the Paradine Plains cactus is a tiny thing that grows only on one particular kind of rock near House Rock Valley on the north rim of the Grand Canyon.

And now there's a new species springing up across Arizona. The communications industry has started disguising its towers as giant cacti. Nobody's given them a name yet but when they do, it'll probably be something like *cellphonius ubiquitious*.

Cacti:

Arizona and cacti are synonymous. Some are real; some are steel; some are cell phone towers.

For centuries, Native Americans have harvested the fruits of various cactus species for use as food and drink. The tradition continues today, with some notable refinements.

The Papago Indians use homemade tools to remove the crimson fruit of the giant saguaro cactus, then convert the figlike pods into jam, candy, syrup, and—for special occasions—wine.

With picking poles made from saguaro skeletons, the women of the tribe rake off the fruit, scoop out the juicy meat, and drop the pod face up on the ground, which, they believe, will entice the rain gods to speed the summer downpours.

Prickly pear fruit is also used to make a variety of edible and potable items, most designed for tourists. Prickly pear jelly and candy are both very sweet and can have a spicy taste. Sometimes only the juice is used as flavoring. The Cerrata Candy Company of Glendale, for example, makes prickly pear and cholla cactus taffy.

Cactus Fruit:

Enjoyed as both food and drink—and as a hangover cure.

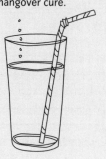

In the summer of 2004, in an article in the *Archives of Internal Medicine,* a group of doctors reported that an extract from the fruit of the prickly pear cactus was effective in fighting hangovers. When taken in capsule form, the substance has been shown to stave off nausea and other aftereffects of overimbibing. In a bit of irony, the Mogollon Brewery of Flagstaff has developed a prickly pear vodka. It's pinkish in color and packs a pretty good wallop.

you know you're in
arizona when ...
... there's a camel on the horizon

Camelback Mountain is a Phoenix-area icon, rising 2,704 feet above sea level and 1,600 feet above the desert and cities that surround it.

Geologically, the peak consists of tilted layers of tertiary red rocks that form a shape resembling the head and hump of a reclining camel facing west. The sandstone conglomerate sits on top of pre-Cambrian granite that may be 1.7 billion years old.

To save the mountain from developers, the city of Phoenix annexed its upper portion and made it into a park. It's a popular hiking spot, with an estimated 300,000 climbers trekking to the top annually. Most of them make it back down safely, but paramedics and helicopters have to rescue several hikers every year. Those who successfully maneuver the 1.2-mile Echo Canyon Trail to the top get a splendid 360-degree view of the Valley of the Sun below.

Camelback Mountain:

The best-known landmark in Phoenix rises 1,600 feet above the desert floor and bears a strong resemblance to a camel's hump.

The park is a favorite among Valley residents, who have bestowed a variety of "best of" honors on it, including "best free attraction," "best park," "best place to hike," and "best place to relieve holiday stress." Not bad for a camel that isn't even a mammal.

you know you're in
arizona when ...
... that wild camel might not be a mirage

There was a time, more than eighty years ago, when people driving across south-western Arizona would stop their vehicles, rub their eyes, and swear off drinking cheap tequila because they thought they had just seen a wild camel.

Actually, they weren't hallucinating. Wild camels were a part of the Arizona landscape for a while because of a military exercise that didn't quite work out. In the 1850s, the Army had survey crews mapping a wagon route along the Thirty-Fifth Parallel in Arizona. Jefferson Davis, then the U.S. Secretary of War, believed camels could help solve the Army's transportation problem, so he imported about sixty animals and a full complement of camel drivers from the Middle East and assigned them to Arizona.

The camels were useful only for a brief time before the survey was finished. The Army sold most of the animals to miners working the area; others were abandoned and left to fend for themselves in the desert.

For several years, camel sightings were not uncommon in portions of the Mohave

Camels:

Wild camels decommissioned from the Army used to roam the Arizona deserts.

Desert in the western part of the state. True, the last confirmed report was in the late 1920s (by a guy who swore he drank nothing stronger than goat's milk), but there may still be some out there . . . .

Old-timers also tell the tale of the Red Ghost, a camel that roamed the desert with the skeleton of a human strapped to its back. So if that camel apparition has a rider apparition, it just might be old Red.

...driving down the street is a yawning experience

Carefree began in 1957 as a place for folks looking to get away from the cares of normal living. People started moving there in earnest in the late 1960s, and the community was incorporated in 1984. Now it has more than 3,000 permanent residents.

The easygoing way of life the founders envisioned is reflected not only in the town's name but also along its streets, where the signs bear such relaxing names as Ho Road and Hum Road, Carefree Drive, Carefree Estates Road, Carefree Mountain Drive, and Carefree Highway.

Elsewhere, there's Easy Street and Calle Facil ("Easy Street" in Spanish). And Dream Street and Drifting Mist Court, Rambling Road and Paint Your Wagon Trail, Serene Street and Whileaway Road, and Nonchalant Avenue and Tranquil Trail.

Also, there's Leisure Court, Leisure Lane, Peaceful Place, Linger Lane, Never Mind Trail, Rocking Chair Road, Breathless Drive, Happy Hollow Drive, Shangri La Lane, Slumber Street, Sleepy Hollow Road, and Sleepy Owl Way.

As well as Tally Ho Drive, This Is It Circle, and No More Road.

Since golf and relaxation are supposed to be partners, Carefree also has Dogleg

Carefree:

The city started as a retirement community and the street names reflect it: There's Ho Road, Hum Road, Easy Street, and Saunter Lane, to name a few.

Drive, Hidden Green Drive, Fairway Trail and Fairway Circle, Lucky Lane, Links Drive, Short Putt Place, Teetime Court, Up and Down Place, Golfcrest Court and Golf Trail, and Yahoo Trail.

Carefree is also home to the Western Hemisphere's largest sundial. It measures 90 feet in diameter with a dial 72 feet long and 4 feet wide. The dial rises 35 feet above the surface of the base. This also fits in with the community's image because the sundial doesn't work between sundown and sunrise or on cloudy days, which gives the townspeople a chance to relax and not worry about what time it is.

you know you're in
arizona when ...
... spelunkers keep secrets

None of Arizona's big caves match those found in Kentucky or Europe in size. Still, they're not bad, considering three of ours are surrounded with bits of intrigue.

Kartchner Caverns near Benson have been open to the public as a state park since 1998 and draw nearly 200,000 visitors per year. But the caves were discovered in 1967 when eighteen-year-old Randy Tufts stumbled across them while hiking in the area. He neither mentioned nor returned to his find until 1974, when he took friend Gary Tenen along. The pair kept their secret until 1978, when they contacted the owners of the land and urged them to protect the caves, which they did by selling it to the state.

Inside the caves, chemical reactions have been going on for millions of years to shape an underground landscape. Here stalagmites and stalactites share space with eerie forms that look like sets from a science fiction movie.

At the Colossal Caves Mountain Park near Tucson, visitors are informed that the underground excavation is a dry limestone cave, that the temperature stays at 70 degrees Fahrenheit, and that there are 363 steps along the route that leads them from start to finish.

But what nobody tells you is where to find the $60,000. Outlaws supposedly hid that much gold within the caverns, but to date, nobody has found it. At least, nobody's saying they found it. It's understandable. Taxes on found gold are extremely high.

The Grand Canyon Caverns east of Seligman aren't nearly as spectacular as these other two, but they do have Gertie the sloth. In her prime as a living creature, Gertie stood about 16 feet tall and weighed about 1,200 pounds. Although not native to her current surroundings, the taxidermied giant stands guard along the pathways. The animal supposedly was found in the caves by early explorers. How it got there is a mystery.

Caves:

Both the Kartchner Caverns and the Colossal Caves feature stalagmites and stalactites and somebody who can tell you the difference. The Grand Canyon Caverns feature Gertie the sloth, who is in a class by herself.

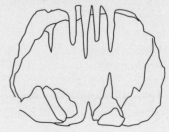

you know you're in
arizona when...
...the cereus blooms

Although much of Arizona is desert, there are a variety of plants that not only thrive in the arid sand but also add touches of beauty. If there has been sufficient rainfall the previous winter, the desert wildflowers blossom from mid-April through late May, creating a palette of color in the desert. Often unnoticed amid the splendor, however, is the ugly duckling of the cactus family, the lowly cereus.

Most of the time—in fact, 364/365ths of the time—the cereus is a less-than-pretty thing with skinny, spiny, grayish-green arms that just lie on the ground not doing much of anything. But, like Cinderella, the plant does have its evening of splendor.

One night a year, sometime between late May and early August, the cereus takes its place in the beauty pageant's winner's circle. The buds appear a couple of days before the extravaganza. They're not much to look at either: just lumpy, green things that pop out of the scrawny arms. But when the big night arrives, the buds open and the air fills with a sweet perfume that

permeates the land for miles. The large white blossoms draw photographers, bees, and botanists in proportionate numbers, and all wait patiently as the petals unfold.

Then it's over. By morning, the flowers are wilted and Cinderella goes back to being a scullery maid. Until next year.

Cereus:

An annual bloomer that gives its all in a single night.

Ed Chilleen started making his own beer after a visit to Europe in 1987. He was so impressed with the beer in Lauf, Germany that he had brewmaster George Arnold design, build, and ship a complete beer-works to Cave Creek, where it was installed and became the Black Mountain Brewing Company.

The brewery is adjacent to the Satisfied Frog restaurant and saloon, also owned by Chilleen and his wife, Maria. They can produce 108,000 gallons a year, which equates to an annual output of more than a million twelve-ounce bottles of brew.

In 1991, Chilleen came up with the idea of dropping a chili into a bottle of pilsner to give it a little extra flavor, and a legend was born. He buys serrano chili peppers from a personally selected grower and pickles them in a secret solution. Each chili is then dropped by hand into a bottle before the bottle is filled with beer.

Chilleen maintains that his is the only chili beer in the world and says he's had to farm out part of his operation to a Minnesota brewery to keep up with the demand.

It's a pretty good beer, but those who consume it in excess face a double dose of pain the next morning—a heartburn hangover.

Chili Beer:

A drinkable liquid that combines hops, malt, burps, and chili peppers. People here accept it; the Japanese buy it by the case.

Code talkers were Navajo Marines who invented a military code that helped win crucial battles in the South Pacific during World War II. The young Navajos used their native tongue to communicate troop movements and orders. Because it was not a written language, the Japanese were unable to decipher it.

To develop the secret vocabulary, they used rough Navajo equivalents to rename military armaments and equipment. For example, they substituted *bird* for *airplane*, *fish* for *ships*, and the Navajo word *egg* for *bomb*.

The code was very difficult to learn, even for the Navajos, and many who tried to become code talkers failed to pass the required testing. The more than 400 who did make it were sworn to secrecy even after the war ended, and they maintained their silence until 1968, when the Defense Department finally declassified their role.

Code Talkers:

During World War II, young Navajo soldiers were instrumental in defeating the Japanese by using their native tongue to send secret messages.

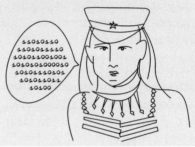

Since then, they have been the subject of several books, some written by the code talkers themselves, and were the heroes in the 2002 movie *Windtalkers*, starring Nicholas Cage. They are also honored by large statues in downtown Phoenix and at the Navajo Veterans Memorial Park in Window Rock, and by a display in a fast food restaurant in Kayenta.

you know you're in
arizona when ...
... cowboys say it just right

Cowboys are usually depicted as tight-lipped ranch hands who "wouldn't say it if they stepped in a pile of it." But some were quite the opposite, ready to utter a colloquialism at the drop of a ten-gallon hat. Many of their sayings have been collected and printed in book form; others were simply passed from generation to generation by the cowhands.

But as housing developments take over cattle ranches in Arizona, cowboy slang is becoming extinct. Before it vanishes forever, here's a sampling of how to say what you really mean, cowboy-style.

"Pretty girls on the frontier are as rare as clean socks in a bunkhouse."

"He's so lazy he won't chew tobacco because then he'd have to spit."

"The water in the Colorado River is too thick to swim in but too thin to plow."

"Cook uses meat so tough you have to use a knife to cut the gravy."

"His boots were so fine you could see the wrinkles in his socks."

"Pull yourself up a piece of ground and I'll cut you off a chunk of that stuff Cookie calls coffee."

"So skinny he'd take five steps before his shadow followed him."

"Whatever donkey you got this whiskey from must've had kidney trouble."

"His coffee tastes like water that was scalded to death."

"The water on his ranch is so thick you have to chew it before swallowing."

Colloquialisms:

Cowboys always mean what they say, but they say it in a peculiar fashion.

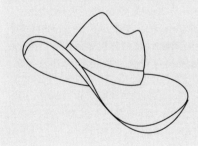

you know you're in
arizona when...
...copper is still king

Some of Arizona's original Big Cs are slowly fading into the sunset: Citrus, cowboys, and cotton are good examples. Others—construction, computers, and Cactus League spring baseball—are gradually replacing them.

But copper maintains its place as a giant in the state's financial picture. Figures for 2003 showed the copper mining industry contributed $2.7 billion to the state's economy and a net of $11.3 billion to the national economy. The Phelps Dodge open pit facility at Morenci covers 50 square miles and produces 20 percent of the nation's copper. It is the sixth-largest copper producer in the world.

An interesting example of copper's prominence in the state's history is a copper dress now in the possession of the Arizona Historical Society in Tucson. Cele Peterson, a Tucson designer and dress shop owner, used layers of leaves cut from woven copper mesh to create the piece. She couldn't use thread to sew the outfit because the copper would have sliced right through it, so she stapled it together.

Those who modeled the dress knew there was a possibility of being nicked and slashed by the twenty-pound dress, and were allowed to wear blue jeans underneath. The creation was introduced to the public at the inaugural Copper Bowl football game held in Tucson in 1989. It's now in storage at the society's museum and can be viewed by appointment only.

Some of the copper mines, however, are open to the public and conduct daily tours. For information, call Phelps Dodge at (877) 646–8687 or visit www.phelpsdodge.com/community-environment. Or contact the Asarco Mineral Discovery Center at (520) 625–7513 or online at www.mineraldiscovery.com.

Copper:

Arizona is still one of the world's leading producers of this metal, which is used in everything from sinks and computers to the occasional fashion statement.

...cowboys don't draw with six-shooters

One wintry night in 1964, three cowboys huddled around a campfire out in the middle of a Mexican desert and shared a bottle of tequila while they plotted their future.

As artists.

The trio consisted of Joe Beeler, Charlie Dye, and John Hampton, all Arizonans who made their living by putting oil on canvas. But they weren't getting rich at it. So on June 23, 1965, they recruited George Phippen of Prescott and held a meeting in a Sedona saloon. It was a historic gathering, especially in art circles, because it marked the beginning of the Cowboy Artists of America.

The founders reckoned that if they organized, they could market their work to a much wider audience. So they established an annual show in Oklahoma City, Oklahoma, where it stayed for seven years before moving to Phoenix in 1973.

Cowboy Artists:

Wranglers armed with paintbrushes are now more popular than gunfighters, thanks to the Cowboy Artists of America, which was organized in Arizona.

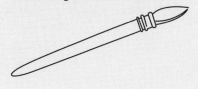

Now the CAA has nearly thirty members, most of them genuine cowboys, all of them artists who deal with the Western image. The annual show's opening night attracts collectors from all over the world, who plunk down nearly $2 million every year to purchase cowboy art.

This is a good example of the benefits of tequila straight from the bottle.

...the cry "Cowboy up!" stops pain faster than aspirin

A 3,000-pound bull unceremoniously deposits a 180-pound cowboy onto the rodeo grounds and then threatens to stomp the ex-rider into the dirt. Or a 160-pound running back gets hammered to the turf by a 300-pound nose tackle. Does either the fallen cowboy or the crumpled halfback get any words of sympathy from his companions?

Nope.

Not in Arizona, at least.

What they get are a mere two words: "Cowboy up!"

Basically, what that means is: "Get up off the ground and show those big guys that you're not scared of them or their big brothers either!"

Some lexicologists trace the origins of the phrase back to the early days of the rodeos, more than a century ago in Arizona. It has long since spread to other forms of endeavor, both on and off the athletic field. Arizona football teams frequently adopt it as a motto, and it's standard bumper sticker literature on in-state pickup trucks. Even the Boston Red Sox borrowed the phrase during the American League baseball playoffs.

It's a good term to incorporate into one's personal terminology, especially when one has just been run down by a pickup truck driven by a linebacker and carrying a large bull.

Cowboy Up:

A two-word pep talk directed at whiners, bull riders who have just been thrown, and anybody else who complains.

you know you're in
arizona when...
...the creosote bush is Public Enemy No. 1

You want to talk about protecting your turf? Take a close look at this killer.

The creosote bush, common to Arizona's deserts, has a unique method of guarding its territory: It kills other plant seedlings that—if allowed to mature—would infringe upon its own growth potential.

Creosote bushes grow in strikingly uniform spacing across the desert, the result of competition for available moisture, of which there isn't very much. The bush's roots give off a toxic substance that kills seedlings.

Although small and scraggly, the bush ties down the desert soil in a defense against the wind and flash floods. The miniature dunes then serve as home sites for toads, lizards, and other creepy-crawly things such as kangaroo rats.

Creosote Bush:

A lowly desert plant with a highly developed system of protecting its own desert turf: It kills the opposition.

And by the way, the creosote bush is not the source of creosote, the wood preservative used to keep railroad ties from rotting. That stuff is a wood tar derived from pine trees. The creosote bush got its name because after a rainfall, it sort of smells like a railroad tie.

you know you're in
arizona when...
...daylight saving time is for sissies

Owners of timepieces in just about every other state have to make twice-a-year adjustments to their chronometers in accordance with the rules laid down by the daylight saving time edicts. Arizona neither springs ahead nor falls back because it's always Mountain Standard Time in the Grand Canyon State. So when Mountain Standard Time switches to Mountain Daylight Time, Arizona technically goes to Pacific Standard Time even though it's still Mountain Standard Time.

And then, to make doubly sure that there's at least some daylight saving time confusion in the state, the Navajo Nation does make the twice-a-year alterations to its clocks.

There have been some attempts to approve the time-shifting process in the state legislature, but each has been met with derision

Daylight Saving Time:

Another hour of sunshine during an Arizona summer? You've got to be kidding!

and defeat. As one veteran lawmaker once put it, "Who in their right mind would want another hour of daytime when it's 111 degrees outside?"

you know you're in
arizona when...
...you have your choice of deserts

There are those, and they are many, who envision Arizona as one big sandbox, an arid land filled with nothing but desert. These observations are always made from afar by nincompoops and illiterates. Well, sure, Arizona does have quite a bit of desert land, but there's a reason.

Arizona's boundaries encompass 113,956 square miles, and an estimated 46,000 of those square miles are considered desert. That's only about 40 percent. But—and this is the good part—it's not just one desert. It's four. No other state can make such a boast, if indeed that's something to boast about.

Arid lands sneak into the state from several directions. Each contains elements common to the other three: sparse rainfall, poisonous snakes, creosote bushes, light vegetation, vermin, and varmints.

The Sonoran Desert occupies the majority of Arizona's land allotted to deserts. It comes up from Mexico and is so big it encompasses two national wildlife ranges, two national monuments dedicated to cactus, and six of the state's largest cities.

Most of the Mohave is in California and Nevada. The section in western Arizona runs along the Colorado River and is the homeland of the Joshua tree forests and record high temperatures.

The Chihuahuan Desert slips into southeastern Arizona from northern Mexico, and is well known for producing century plants that shoot tall, narrow spikes skyward in remarkably short time periods. The Chiricahua Mountains rise abruptly from the floor of the Chihuahuan Desert, and about 80 percent of the nation's snakebite serum comes from this desert's wildlife.

When the Great Basin Desert wanders into northeastern Arizona, it has already traveled across six other states. Huge petrified trees, Canyon de Chelly, the Painted Desert, portions of the Navajo Nation, and giant sandstone formations mark its presence in the state.

Deserts:

Arizona is arid and dry for a reason: It's the only state that has four deserts within its boundaries.

you know you're in
arizona when ...
... dil is part of your holiday feast

Some members of the Navajo Nation consider dil a delicacy, but it's not for everyone, especially the squeamish. *Dil* is the tribal name for blood sausage, and it's usually served as a side dish to turkey and ham during the holiday season.

The sausage is a mixture of diced potatoes, celery, sheep fat, onion, cornmeal, salt, and pepper combined with fresh sheep blood. The filling is stuffed into a sheep belly bag and boiled outdoors. The process is part of the traditional sheep butchering.

Dil is often served as a welcoming gesture to a family member who has been away from the reservation for a long time. Like, a blood relative.

Dil:

It's considered a delicacy by some, but you have to have the stomach for it.

you know you're in
arizona when...
...dinosaurs stomp along Route 66

Long before Sir Richard Attenborough's *Jurassic Park* movies, dinosaurs were already in service as marketing tools in and around Holbrook. Although the city has a Wild West history, and the fabled Route 66 once ran directly through downtown, it's the dinosaurs that get the most attention.

They're not real, of course. The last of the big, bad boys disappeared a long, long time ago. But more than 225 million years ago, during the Triassic Period, the high tableland surrounding the city was a vast floodplain populated by small dinosaurs, huge reptiles, and fish-eating amphibians. Today they're cast in concrete and sent out to attract the tourists.

They line the freeways and city streets. At Stewarts Petrified Wood along Interstate 40, a green dinosaur snarfs down a department store mannequin, another attacks a bus, and a pterodactyl hovers over a building. Up the freeway a few miles, a realistic-looking tyrannosaurus rex gobbles up a lesser creature to draw the attention of passersby to the Dinosaur Park, International Petrified Forest, and Museum of the Americas. The combined establishment has several fake prehistorics along the roadway and a real dinosaur leg bone in the museum.

In downtown Holbrook, dinosaurs serve as both art and signage. Two oversize carnivores guard the entrance at Petrified Rock Garden, and a family of giant green monsters stands in front of the Rainbow Rock Shop. Just around the corner, Julien's Roadrunner sells dinosaur T-shirts, dinosaur license plates, dinosaur bumper stickers, and old Sinclair Oil signs that feature a brontosaurus.

A city park also has a dinosaur as its centerpiece. It's a 6-foot tall bronze sculpture of an unnamed species that was donated to Holbrook by a man who bought it in New York.

Dinosaurs:

Along Route 66, they're not just movie stars; they're also marketing tools.

you know you're in
arizona when ...
... "dry heat" is a permanent part of the language

From late May until mid-October, when daytime temperatures in the desert frequently reach and often surpass 100 degrees Fahrenheit, veteran Arizonans utilize two methods of dealing with it:

First, flee to the state's mountains or the California coast.

Second, bear in mind that it's a dry heat.

Since only the privileged few can spend the entire summer in the hills or on the water, the second option is so popular that the term "but it's a dry heat" has become Arizona's unofficial motto. It would be the official motto if *Ditat Deus* ("God Enriches") hadn't been selected by legislators in an air-conditioned office. The unofficial motto may be used to belittle those who think that 110 degrees is going to fry their brains, as in, "Well of course it's hot. You're in the desert. But it's a dry heat."

Others use such logic as, "But it's a dry heat. Think of how much you'd be sweating if it was this hot in Georgia," or "Thank your lucky stars that it's a dry heat. If it wasn't, we'd be spending a fortune on underarm deodorant." It is also the front line of defense against Midwesterners who call every summer to ask if it's hot enough for us. They are the same people we call every winter to inquire whether it's cold enough for them.

While summertime temperatures soar well above 100 degrees, humidity is well below 40 percent most of the time. This gives the dry heat theorem credibility. But credibility does not prevent sunburn, steering wheel burns, thirst, and droopy underwear, all side effects of the heat, dry or not.

For the record, the hottest it's ever been in Arizona was 128 degrees, registered at Lake Havasu City on June 29, 1994. The hottest day in Phoenix was 122 degrees on June 26, 1990. That mark is noteworthy because:

1. It's easy to remember by simply adding the digits in 6/26/90, which total 122.

2. It was so hot that all flights at Sky Harbor Airport in Phoenix were grounded because the heat affected the instruments.

3. It was a dry heat.

Dry Heat:

The phrase "but it's a dry heat" should be Arizona's motto—it's used far more often than the state's official phrase.

you know you're in
arizona when ...
... rivers run dry

Only a few Arizona rivers actually have water in them. The others, for much of the time, are more navigable by sand buggies than by boat. This tidbit of information was a major reason why an escape plan hatched by German prisoners of war didn't work.

During the latter stages of World War II, as many as 400 German prisoners of war were housed in the Papago Park internment camp in Phoenix. On December 23, 1944, twenty-five of them escaped through a tunnel they had dug during the previous three months. The tunnel went 14 feet down, then another 180 feet to the Crosscut Canal. Three prisoners had constructed a rudimentary boat that they dragged through the tunnel because, according to the maps they had secured, the Salt River was a short distance away. Once they reached the Salt River, they assumed, they could navigate their way to the Colorado River and then down to Mexico.

But although they were veteran seafarers who had served on U-boats, the Germans didn't know about Arizona's sandy rivers. Their maps delineated the rivers in blue, like most maps do, but blue in Arizona

Dry Rivers:

Arizona's rivers frequently don't have water in them, and that once foiled a prison break.

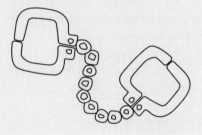

doesn't necessarily mean water will be present. And so, when the escapees reached the Salt River, they found nothing but rocks and sand.

Most of the prisoners either returned to the compound of their own accord or were recaptured. One came back because he didn't want to miss Christmas dinner. Another surrendered to a woman hanging her laundry out to dry. Their leader, Capt. Jurgen Wattenberg, remained on the loose until the following spring, when a service station attendant noted his German accent as he asked how to get to the train station.

you know you're in
arizona when ...
... the "Fab Five" isn't a rock group

In November 1997, five Arizona women were elected to the top five positions in state government, the first time anything like that had happened in the history of the United States.

Jane Dee Hull became the state's first elected female governor. Betsy Bayless won the race for secretary of state. Janet Napolitano was voted in as attorney general; Carol Springer won the state treasurer's spot; and Lisa Graham Keegan was elected superintendent of public instruction.

The women drew national attention when both local and national media started calling them the "Fab Five." Their notoriety also got a boost when they were featured in *People* and *George* magazine articles.

Since then, Napolitano was elected governor. She appointed Bayless to head her department of administration. Hull was selected as a delegate to the United Nations by Pres. George W. Bush; Keegan went to Washington, D.C., as head of the Education Leaders Conference; and Springer was elected to the Yavapai County Board of Supervisors.

Fab Five:

A quintet of women politicians who grabbed all the brass rings.

you know you're in
arizona when ...
... flash floods can be deadly

Despite its arid reputation, Arizona is often the site of killer flash floods that sweep across the desert with deadly force, destroying everything in their way.

They are the fastest-moving type of flood, and they occur when heavy rain collects in streams, washes, and arroyos, turning the usually dry channels into raging torrents. Because they happen so quickly and move so rapidly, flash floods catch many people off guard. They have the power to move boulders, tear down trees, destroy buildings, and obliterate bridges with walls of water as high as 20 feet.

Since much of Arizona is desert, the land is hardened by endless days of blistering heat. So when rainfall does occur, the ground can't absorb it. And with little vegetation to hold it back, the runoff gathers force and goes just about anywhere it wants.

Three tragic examples in August 1997 illustrate the dangers associated with the phenomenon. On August 6, a flash flood in a wash near Douglas killed six illegal immigrants. Four days later, a flash flood near Kingman derailed an Amtrak passenger

Flash Floods:

When rain falls it comes in a hurry, but because the ground is hard from being so dry it doesn't soak it up—so it runs down the arroyos and washes in floods.

train, injuring 150 passengers. Two days after that, eleven European tourists were swept to their deaths when a distant thunderstorm produced a flash flood that raced through Antelope Canyon where they were hiking.

Weather experts warn that even ankle-deep water is a threat in an arroyo, and less than two feet of rushing floodwater can carry away an automobile.

The World's Sometimes Tallest Fountain in Fountain Hills shoots a stream of recycled water more than 500 feet straight up. It shot its first water rocket on December 15, 1970, and at one time ran for fifty-five minutes of every hour. But today, due to economic and ecological concerns, it runs for only fifteen minutes every hour between 9:00 A.M. and 9:00 P.M. year round.

The Fountain Hills fountain was unchallenged as the world's tallest spouter until the mid-1990s, when it lost the title to the Gateway Geyser in East St. Louis, Illinois, which shoots a stream 627 feet into the air. However, the Illinois geyser operates only from mid-April through mid-October so, like the one in Fountain Hills, it can lay claim to the title of being the world's tallest fountain only part of the time.

The Fountain Hills fountain is the world's tallest on such special occasions as St. Patrick's Day (when the water is colored green) and New Year's Day. On those days, all three pumps are operational, propelling a stream of water 560 feet toward the heavens; the rest of the time only two

Fountain:

Some days it's the world's tallest fountain; other times it slips all the way to fourth place. But this Arizona icon is capable of shooting a jet of water more than 500 feet straight up.

pumps are working so they only shoot a 330-foot stream. Fountains in Switzerland and Australia also surpass that output, shooting jets of 400 and 450 feet, respectively.

But the folks in Fountain Hills don't mind settling for having the World's Tallest Fountain West of the Mississippi.

you know you're in
arizona when...
... you can be in three other states at the same time

Four Corners Monument is located at the very tip of northeastern Arizona. And the very tip of southwestern Colorado. And the very tip of northwestern New Mexico. And the very tip of southeastern Utah.

Each state's boundaries runs smack-dab into the other three at that point, making it the only place in the nation where people can stand in four states at the same time. The original monument was a small concrete slab set in place in 1912, the year Arizona and New Mexico became states. That first piece of concrete was replaced with a larger slab with the borderlines etched into it. A strategically placed observation tower lets people take photographs of their loved ones contorting themselves to properly align their hands and feet into a quad-state position.

The area is on the Navajo Reservation, and guests who finally get themselves untwisted can purchase traditional food and jewelry on the site. The federal government is in the process of upgrading the area to provide better facilities for both visitors and vendors. The project should be finished by late 2005.

Four Corners:

The only place in the United States where being in four states at the same time is not only possible, it's done all the time.

If they could do it, the ghosts of Arizona's ghost towns would probably trace their ancestry back to the mining industry, which created new towns when times were good, boomtowns when the money was rolling in, and then ghost towns when the mines failed.

The towns were given names like Ruby, Gleeson, Pearce, Stanton, Kentucky Camp, Klondyke, and Silverbell, and in their hey-days they had thousands of residents. But not anymore.

Today they are reminders of times past. Ruby is a good example. Those who study such things rate it as the best ghost town in the Southwest. Ruby was founded in the 1870s and named after the wife of the first postmaster. The town went through a bloody period, with four people murdered in the same store during the 1920s. But by 1936, it had about 2,000 residents, and the town's Montana Mine was Arizona's leading producer of lead and zinc and third in silver production.

The ore played out around 1940 and in less than a year, Ruby was deserted. Today the town has about twenty buildings still standing but deteriorating. And since nobody

lives there, nobody's sure if any ghosts reside there, but it does look like the kind of place they'd hang out. If there are such things as ghosts, that is.

But even though there's not much to see there (the rumored ghosts are very shy and rarely make public appearances), Ruby remains a popular attraction for both tourists and those who like to poke around in what used to be. For those who just have to go there, it's in western Santa Cruz County.

Ghost Towns:

The mines came and went, but the old towns stayed behind, occupied now only by things that go *bump* in the night.

RUBY SALOON

Nobody has ever actually met Abby Byr or Oatie. Not in person, anyway. Even hotel guests who claim they've had run-ins with them are hesitant to talk about the encounters because Abby and Oatie are two of Arizona's more famous ghosts.

Or so they say.

Abby Byr and her husband once owned the Hotel Vendome in Prescott. They lost it for unpaid taxes, but the new owners graciously allowed them to stay in Room 16. One night Abby became ill and sent her husband out for medicine. He never returned. Disconsolate, Abby took to her bed, refused to eat or drink, and died. According to the legend, her faithful cat Noble also perished at the same time.

But there are those who claim that Abby and Noble still roam the hallways and pester the guests, especially those who occupy Room 16. A book in the hotel lobby contains testimonials from people who recount sudden breezes, the scent of a strong perfume, rattling doors, meowing sounds, and ghostly shapes.

The stories say Oatie was an Irish miner who came to Oatman during its boom days. After saving up enough money, he sent for his sweetheart back in Ireland, but she never showed up. Despondent, the young man wasted away and died one night in an alley behind the Oatman Hotel.

Ghosts:

In Arizona, ghosts hang around old hotels and trouble some of the guests, but they're harmless.

But some believe Oatie is still hanging around. Hotel guests have reported seeing the outline of his body on a bed in his old room, a quilt floating down the hall, and a rocking chair rocking with no one seated in it. He is also blamed for shattered glasses in the bar and the sound of bodies being dragged down the hallway.

Those who don't mind having ghosts as bed partners might also check out the Hotel Monte Vista in Flagstaff, San Carlos Hotel in Phoenix, Oliver House Bed and Breakfast in Bisbee, Red Garter Bakery and Breakfast in Williams, the Cochise Hotel in Cochise, and the Acadia Hotel in Oracle. There are, according to those who believe in such things, ghosts in all of them.

There are only two poisonous lizards in the world. One of them—the gila monster—lives in Arizona. The other is the beaded lizard of Mexico, a close relative.

Although poisonous, gila monsters are not considered dangerous. For one thing, they're extremely rare and reclusive. For another, they are reluctant to bite and generally do so only when they have been provoked. Where rattlesnakes and other more common forms of death-dealing reptiles deliver their poisons through syringe-like fangs, the gila monster has grooved teeth that dispense the venom. When it does bite, the creature hangs on like a pit bull, allowing the poison to work its way through the teeth into the wound.

Gila monsters are protected by the state Game and Fish Department, which doles out severe penalties to anyone killing or catching one. Unfortunately, the creatures are often captured and offered as exotic pets because of their coral-and-black scales that resemble Indian beadwork.

Gila Monsters:

One of only two poisonous lizards in the world, this monster is slow but deadly.

There is no record of anyone in Arizona dying from a gila monster bite, but there is an unsubstantiated legend about such a case. Seems these two good old boys were out drinking and they got into an argument. When one passed out, the other grabbed a gila monster that just happened to be hanging around their campfire, opened its jaws, and clamped them down on his rival's arm. The victim died; the killer was arrested and found guilty of murder by gila monster.

Or so the story goes.

you know you're in
arizona when...
...a river guide can become Mr. Arizona

Barry Goldwater and Arizona are synonymous. The son of a pioneering family, Goldwater rose to national prominence as a U.S. Senator and presidential candidate. His public service and his varied career earned him the honorary name "Mr. Arizona."

In his early days, he was, among other things, a high school class president who flunked most of his subjects; a riverboat guide in the Grand Canyon; a storekeeper; one of the state's first ham radio operators; a respected photographer; and a World War II pilot. After the war, he organized the Arizona Air National Guard, won a seat on the Phoenix City Council, and rose to political heights.

He was elected to the U.S. Senate in 1952 and ran for president against Lyndon B. Johnson in 1964. He served in the Senate for thirty years (1952–64 and 1968–86) and gained worldwide attention for his conservative politics, the subject of his best-selling book, *Conscience of a Conservative.*

One of Goldwater's photographs was the first color cover for the prestigious *Arizona Highways* magazine, which printed about 200 of his pictures. His skill with a camera earned him a membership in the Royal Photographic Society of London.

Goldwater's popularity and blunt style of politics were credited with increasing the Republican Party's power in the West and South. He died in 1998 at age eighty-nine and is memorialized by a life-size sculpture in a park on the corner of Tatum Boulevard and Lincoln Drive in Paradise Valley.

Ironically, Goldwater's first national attention came from men's underwear, not politics. While operating the family store in 1938, he introduced a line of men's shorts adorned with large red ants. He called them "Antsy Pants," and the store was besieged with orders from across the nation.

Barry Goldwater:

A Renaissance man who influenced Republican politics.

you know you're in
arizona when...
...you can both ski and golf in January

According to the Arizona Golf Association's latest figures, there are 338 golf courses in Arizona. More than 180 of them are in the Phoenix area.

The state also has four ski resorts, none of them in the Phoenix area. But there is one near Tucson, about 120 miles south of Phoenix: the Ski Valley Resort atop Mount Lemmon, the southernmost ski facility in the nation. The other three are the Snow Bowl in the San Francisco Peaks at Flagstaff (about 140 miles north of Phoenix), the Williams Ski Area (about 40 miles west of Flagstaff), and Sunrise in the White Mountains near Greer (about 250 miles northeast of Phoenix).

Tucson also has twenty-six golf courses.

What that means is that in the winter months, those interested can use either Phoenix or Tucson as a base and, if they so desire, play golf in the morning and ski in the afternoon. Or vice versa.

And for the really hardy, there's also water skiing as a winter sport. Saguaro Lake and Lake Pleasant, both only a few miles from Phoenix, are ideal venues for skimming across the water on flat boards.

Golf:

This popular sport is not the only form of outdoor recreation in Arizona during the winter months.

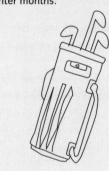

George Wiley Paul Hunt came to the Arizona Territory in 1881 to prospect for gold but found his fortune in politics. After the Territory became a state, he was elected to the state's highest office so often that he became known as "Arizona's hereditary governor."

Hunt, a Democrat, won his first term shortly after Arizona achieved statehood in 1912. He served until 1919, then again from 1923 to 1929, then once more from 1931 to 1933. Despite his apparent popularity, Hunt wasn't always the clear-cut favorite.

In 1916 Republican challenger Tom Campbell apparently beat Hunt by thirty votes. Hunt contested the election, and both men were sworn in as governor in separate ceremonies on January 1, 1917. Hunt refused to vacate the governor's office, so Campbell set up headquarters in the kitchen of his own home.

Things got worse. The state treasurer and the state auditor, both Democrats, refused to honor checks signed by Campbell. Both governors addressed the state legislature when it convened. A Superior Court judge ruled that Campbell had indeed won by twenty votes. But that was not the last word on the five-month legal battle.

Later that year, the State Supreme Court reversed the Superior Court decision and declared Hunt the winner by forty-three votes. The Supreme Court also ordered the state to pay Hunt's salary for the entire year, but gave Campbell nothing.

The episode set a precedent for future Arizona gubernatorial wackiness. From 1975 through 1997, only one elected governor completed a full term. Raul Castro, elected in 1974, resigned to become U.S. ambassador to Argentina. Wesley Bolin, appointed to succeed Castro, died five months after taking office. Atty. Gen. Bruce Babbitt served the remainder of the Castro/Bolin term, then was re-elected twice. Evan Mecham was elected in 1986 but impeached by the state senate. Sec. of State Rose Mofford completed Mecham's term but didn't run again. Fife Symington was elected in 1990 and 1994 but resigned in 1997 after being convicted of defrauding investors prior to his election. Sec. of State Jane Hull completed his term, then opted not to run in 2002.

Governors:

Getting elected governor of Arizona doesn't guarantee job security.

43

you know you're in
arizona when ...
... you can drive to the Grand Canyon anytime you feel like it

The longest gorge in the world is the Grand Canyon, a 290-mile-long slash that cuts its way across the Colorado Plateau in northern Arizona. It's a mile deep and 18 miles from one rim to the other at its widest point. And even when it narrows, it's still 10 miles across.

The canyon is the product of erosion, most of it caused by the Colorado River, which, even after millions of years, still flows through its creation. Although tamed somewhat by dams and diversion projects, the Colorado follows the same path it established some six million years ago, when it first made a major course alteration. Wind, rain, snow, heat, cold, and hundreds of tributaries that flow into the canyon have all helped the erosion process.

Grand Canyon:

The world's largest gorge has been formed over six million years by the Colorado River, wind, rain, extreme temperatures, and other forms of erosion.

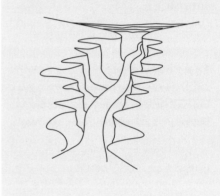

But the magic of the canyon is not in cold, hard figures. It is an ever-changing entity, its beauty enhanced every day by sunlight and shadows and by the clouds that occasionally drift down into its depths, covering the spires, hues, and strata below. As explorer John Wesley Powell wrote after traversing the canyon in 1869, "You cannot see the Grand Canyon in one view, as if it were a changeless spectacle from which a curtain might be lifted."

More than five million people flock to the canyon every year, most of them armed with the latest photographic equipment, most of them destined to be disappointed when their pictures don't capture the place's magnificence and splendor. But for many, it's a rare opportunity to stand in awe, peer over the edge, and look a mile straight down.

Still others, however, are more technically minded, asking such questions as, "How long did it take them to dig that?" and "Is there an escalator that goes to the bottom?"

you know you're in
arizona when ...
... you know why Zane Grey rode away

Zane Grey originally studied dentistry but abandoned that pursuit and took up writing as a full-time career. He came to Arizona in 1907 and was fascinated by the rugged landscape and the rugged people who scraped out a living on it. After touring the north rim of the Grand Canyon on horseback, he produced his first book, a nonfiction work titled *The Last of the Plainsman.*

In 1912 Grey published perhaps his most famous novel, *Riders of the Purple Sage.* It was his first attempt at fiction and became a standard for western novels. The book was made into a movie by the same name in 1930 and has been remade twice since. He followed that success by writing more than eighty other books that were instrumental in propagating the myth of the Arizona cowboy.

Grey built a lodge in the Tonto Basin area and returned to the state regularly to hunt with friends. But in 1929 he was denied a permit to hunt for bear. Angered by the refusal, he left the state in a huff and vowed never to return. He kept his promise, but his legacy remains. His books are still big sellers and his lodge was a tourist attraction until a forest fire destroyed it in 1990. A reproduction is now under construction in Payson.

Zane Grey:

A prolific author of western novels, Grey's most famous works sprung from images he gathered while living in Arizona. But he left the state in a huff because of a bear.

you know you're in
arizona when ...
... it's still high noon at the O.K. Corral

On October 26, 1881, Wyatt Earp, his brothers Morgan and Virgil, and their crony Doc Holliday strode down a Tombstone street toward the O.K. Corral, where they would face Ike Clanton, his son Billy, and brothers Frank and Tom McLaury in a showdown that had been brewing for months.

Within the next thirty seconds or so, several shots were fired and four of the participants were wounded, three of them mortally. Both McLaury brothers and Billy Clanton died at the scene; Morgan Earp took a bullet in the leg. Then it was over.

Well, not really.

Ever since that day, the Gunfight at the O.K. Corral has been analyzed, scrutinized, and immortalized by scholars, historians, and moviemakers. All have drawn their own conclusions, but most depict the Earps and Holliday as the good guys. Others maintain that the trio bullied the Clanton gang into an unfair shootout and should have been convicted of murder.

Exhibits in the Tombstone Courthouse State Historic Park try to portray what actually happened, but museum officials admit there could be flaws in both of the versions presented.

Hollywood, however, does not let such factual inconsistencies stand in the way of a good movie. The gunfight has been the subject of several classic productions, including *My Darling Clementine, Gunfight at the O.K. Corral, Tombstone, Hour of the Gun,* and *Wyatt Earp*. All contended that theirs was the truest version. Many dispute the claims.

Portraying Wyatt Earp has provided temporary work for such actors as Henry Fonda, Kevin Costner, James Garner, Hugh O'Brian, Guy Madison, Joel McCrea, Richard Dix, James Stewart, Randolph Scott, Burt Lancaster, and Kurt Russell. Victor Mature, Val Kilmer, Dennis Quaid, Cesar Romero, Kirk Douglas, Jason Robards, Stacy Keach, Walter Huston, and Kent Taylor have all portrayed Doc Holliday.

The legend is also carried on by regular reenactments on the main streets of Tombstone, particularly during the tourist season.

Gunfight:

The shootout at the O.K. Corral in Tombstone lasted only thirty seconds, but it has taken on a life of its own.

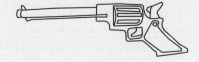

...a tilde can hurt

The habanero is a pepper. A very hot pepper. A sneaky, rotten little pepper that's so hot it can start an avalanche. Despite that, it is a very popular ingredient in many dishes served in Arizona, particularly salsa.

Although the dictionary makes no distinction between *habanero* and *habañero,* with the little wavy line called a *tilde* over the *n,* there are many who claim the tilde makes a big difference. Veteran cooks who prepare Mexican food—particularly those who cook at home with old family recipes—are very specific about the matter. They warn that a tilded *habañero* is much more powerful than one without the wavy line.

According to them, *habanero* without the tilde is pronounced "ha-ba-NER-o." Add the tilde and it's "ha-ba-NYER-o." That is a lot of power to be placed in the hands of a little wavy line. Think of what could happen if the tildes ever got organized and started showing up in every word with an *n* in it. For example, *bañaña* would then be pronounced "ban-YAN-ya" and give the vocal cords a major surprise.

But it gets worse. Spelled without the tilde, the habanero is capable of causing stomach upset, intestinal revolution, and gastronomic landslides. By placing the tilde over

the *n,* you bestow a power sort of like what happens when newsboy Billy Batson becomes Captain Marvel by uttering "Shazam!" because it gives the pepper super strength. Once tilded, the habañero can melt cast iron. If a group of tilded habañeros were to invade Greenland, they'd turn it into a sandy wasteland.

Basically, the word means "from Havana." However, most who encounter a habanero of either species have several other translations, most of them unusable in proper company.

Habaneros:

Cruel little peppers designed to cause pain and agony for the unwary; they get even worse when a tilde is placed over the *n.*

Etymologically speaking, haboobs are immi-grants. Many years ago they roamed the southern edge of the Sahara and had never even heard of Arizona. But with the advance of technology and media weather forecasters, they've made the leap across continents.

Haboobs are best described as hot, strong winds usually associated with large dust storms, sandstorms, and small tornadoes. They can last as long as three hours and are most common during summer. Because they usually occur in arid places, they can transport huge quantities of sand or dust as they move along at speeds of up to fifteen miles per hour.

Arizona had dust storms long before humans arrived, but they went relatively unnoticed until civilization advanced. Before the mid-1980s, they were merely called sandstorms or dust storms. But when weather reporters in the state observed that these storms were the same things as those in Africa, and that *haboob* is a much more exotic word than *sandstorm,* the term became part of the language.

Regardless of what they're called, haboobs (or sandstorms or dust storms) are mighty

Haboobs:

Every year around August, the monsoons storm across Arizona, bringing huge sandstorms known as *haboobs* with them.

spectacles. They form in the deserts of northern Mexico and southern Arizona, then gather strength and tons of dirt, grit, and sand as they move north. By the time they get to Phoenix, these awesome clouds of dust can stretch miles across and rise thousands of feet above the desert floor.

Drivers who get caught in a haboob often find the visibility reduced to zero, a factor that frequently causes chain-reaction multi-vehicle pileups, particularly on Interstate 10 between Tucson and Phoenix.

The original Hashknife Gang was formed in the late 1880s, during a turbulent and violent period in Arizona's history. The members were cowhands who worked for the Aztec Land and Cattle Company in the northeastern part of the state. The company bought one million acres of former railroad grant land for fifty cents an acre, and when it started operation, it was the third largest cattle outfit in North America.

At one point, the spread was 650 miles long and as much as 80 miles wide. The Hashknife Gang took its name from the company's brand, which resembled the hash knife used by ranch cooks to cut meat and vegetables. Many of the cowhands were also enterprising cattle rustlers, and some of them started their own ranches with cattle stolen from their bosses.

The Aztec Company went out of business in 1900 following a blizzard that killed thousands of cows. The gang was relegated to the history books until 1955, when the new version was formed as a search-and-rescue operation in the White Mountains. The mail-carrying concept was added in 1958, and

now about two dozen riders mount up in Holbrook every February and ride more than 200 miles to Scottsdale, carrying an estimated 20,000 pieces of mail in their saddlebags.

Each piece of mail is stamped with a special cachet to inform the recipient that it was borne by the Pony Express, and the riders arrive in Scottsdale in time to take part in the annual Parada del Sol parade and rodeo.

Hashknife Riders:

Once a year they saddle up and carry the mail.

Yes, my friends, there still are places where you can get away from it all. Well, most of it anyway. One is Havasu Canyon, a beautiful piece of scenery about 35 miles west of the Grand Canyon. It is filled with waterfalls, lush vegetation, and sparkling blue waters. Equally important, not many people go there.

The reason: The Havasupai Indians, who own the property, decided years ago not to allow road construction in the canyon. That eliminated cars, trucks, tour buses, and four-wheelers, and their respective passengers. So the only means of access are foot power, horseback, or atop of a mule. Since it's more than 10 miles to the bottom, it's also more than 10 miles back to the top, and every step of the trip out of the canyon is a steep uphill climb. Mercifully, helicopter flights are now allowed to bring the weak-of-knee and pot-of-belly out. (It's expensive, but for those who misjudge their hiking abilities, it's either fly out or stay forever.)

The waterfalls of Havasu Canyon are Arizona's finest. Navajo Falls is a series of smaller cascades that drop 75 feet into ponds below. Havasu Falls plunge 100 feet into an aqua-colored pool surrounded by travertine deposits. The most spectacular is Mooney Falls, a 196-foot column of water that the early Havasupais called Mother of the Waters. Sadly, it's now named after a white prospector who died there.

Supai Village, located on the trail about halfway down, is home to most of the 500 to 600 members of the Havasupai Tribe. It is the most remote village in the United States. The nearest grocery store is 160 miles away, and the mail and supplies are still delivered by pack mule.

Havasu Canyon:

Pristine waterfalls, secret hideaways, and an Indian village are all found at the bottom of Havasu Canyon—but getting there can be a challenge.

you know you're in
arizona when ...
. . . you think of Iwo Jima

On February 23, 1945, photographer Joe Rosenthal snapped a picture of six military men raising an American flag over Iwo Jima, a small island in the South Pacific. The photo was distributed by the Associated Press and became an instant classic, a symbol of American determination in the waning days of World War II.

Three of the men pictured died on Iwo Jima. The survivors handled the fame in different ways. John Bradley kept his participation a secret. Rene Gagnon tried to capitalize on it but failed. And Ira Hayes became a martyr.

Hayes was a Pima Indian who spent most of his life in Bapchule on the Gila River Indian Reservation. After high school he enlisted in the Marines, then was sent to Iwo Jima and infamy. The flag shown in the photo was the second to be raised that day. A Marine commander had decided the first one was too small, so he sent a squad back up Mount Suribachi to put up the one Rosenthal photographed.

The picture rejuvenated a war-weary nation and became the catalyst for a huge fund-raising drive. The three survivors were taken out of their units and sent on a national tour that eventually produced $2 billion for the war effort. But Hayes was a

Ira Hayes:

A reluctant hero who helped raise the flag on Iwo Jima but paid a severe price for his moment of fame.

reluctant hero. Shy and unassuming, he was forced to become a celebrity and had difficulty handling the fame. Unable to deal with the large crowds of well-wishers who thrust outstretched hands and drinks toward him, Hayes started down a path that led to alcoholism and fifty-five arrests for drunkenness. He died in 1955 at age thirty-two. A Phoenix newspaper eulogized: "Ira Hayes was a victim of war as surely as though he had died on Iwo Jima with his buddies. The peace he fought to win never brought him personal peace. But he is no less a hero for that. Arizona will always honor his memory and the proud symbol he helped create."

you know you're in
arizona when...
...the trading post still trades

The floor creaks inside the Hubbell Trading Post at Ganado, creating a suitable atmosphere for those who visit. The creaking floor is a prelude to the whispers and hushed tones of respect that such a venerable place deserves.

A National Historic Site and the oldest continuously operating trading post in the Navajo Nation, the post was constructed in 1883 using huge stones from the surrounding area. It still looks much like it did in the nineteenth century. There have been some additions and alterations but most have complemented the original buildings.

John Lorenzo Hubbell started the post, where he traded staples and other merchandise for Navajo wool, sheep, rugs, jewelry, and pottery. He died in 1930, but his family continued the operation until 1967, when the National Park Service bought the property.

Hubbell Trading Post:

One of the few remnants of a time when bartering was a way of life.

The post still provides basic services to residents of Ganado, offering everything from canned beans to soda. Equally important, it still has rooms where Navajo artisans can display and sell their wares. Although it's still a trading post, barter is no longer considered legal tender. But cash and credit cards are readily accepted.

you know you're in
arizona when...
...you make reservations for reservations

The first peoples of Arizona were the Anasazi, Hohokam, Mogollon, and Salado, the ancestors of the present Indians who reside in the state. The ancient cultures had living populations in the area when the Spanish explored the Southwest in the 1500s.

Like their forefathers, many Native Americans are still engaged in agriculture. But unlike those who came before, the tribes have diversified. Today their major industries include mining, gaming, tourism and recreation, hotels and motels, timber, golf, land leasing, and arts and crafts.

The twenty-three Indian reservations in the state range in size from the sprawling Navajo Nation—the largest in the United States, covering 29,817 square miles and portions of four states—to the Pascua-Yaqui Reservation of 1,152 acres.

Reservations in the south are the Cocopah, Fort Yuma-Quechan, Pascua-Yaqui, San Xavier, Colorado River, and the Tohono O'odham Nation.

In the north are the Havasupai, Hualapai, Fort Mohave, Hopi, Navajo, Zuni Pueblo, and Kaibab-Paiute.

Reservations in the central portion of the state include Ak Chin, Gila Bend, Yavapai-Apache, Yavapai-Prescott, Salt River Pima-Maricopa, Fort McDowell Yavapai, San Carlos Apache, Gila River, Tonto Apache, and White Mountain Apache.

As part of their tourism efforts, many of the tribes offer overnight lodging in hotels, motels, and campgrounds. You can contact them through the Arizona Office of Tourism at (888) 520–3434 or www.arizona guide.com.

And yes, you do need reservations.

Indian Reservations:

Arizona contains twenty-three Indian tribal reservations within its borders. Some are huge; others are the size of a small town.

Other states apply rather plain-sounding names to their Indian ruins, like Chaco Canyon in New Mexico and Mesa Verde in Colorado. Arizona, on the other hand, uses names that flow off the tongue with such fanciful sounds that they command the speaker to utter them again and again until they become a nonsensical song.

The two primary mouth-delighters are Wupatki and Tuzigoot. Wupatki and Tuzigoot. Mairzy doats and dozey doats. See how it gets to you?

Actually, both sites are great places to visit—colorful, photogenic, and historic. They were established around A.D. 1100, by peoples now called Anasazi and Sinagua. Wupatki stands on the barren plains of the Great Basin Desert northeast of Flagstaff; Tuzigoot rises above the floor of the Verde Valley near Clarkdale.

Archaeologists say the Wupatki Pueblo once housed as many as one hundred people. The buildings fit perfectly into the landscape, with the red sandstone outcrop as a backbone and stone rooms crafted out of blocks. Wupatki (Hopi for "something long that has been cut") was discovered in 1851 but left unattended until 1924, when it was declared a national monument.

Tuzigoot takes its name from an Apache word meaning "crooked water." It is the remnant of a Sinagua village built between A.D. 1125 and 1400. The original limestone and sandstone pueblo was two stories high, but archaeologists speculate that there was no original floor plan. The building simply grew, add-on by add-on, as the population increased. The small cluster of rooms probably contained up to fifty inhabitants.

Since the people who lived there didn't give the ruins their current names, they never knew the joy of repeating them aloud. But today's visitors can say them over and over until they dance around the brain and leave an impression that never goes away.

Woo-PAT-ki. WOO-pat-ki. TOO-zee-goot. Too-ZEE-goot.

Catchy.

Indian Ruins:

The state has several well-preserved ruins, but some of them are worth visiting just because of the way their names sound when they roll off your tongue.

Woo-PAT-ki
WOO-pAt-Ki
TOO-zee-Goot
Too-ZEE-Goot

you know you're in
arizona when ...
... kachinas watch over you

From the beginning, *kachina* has meant three things to the Hopi—a spirit they believe in, a masked impersonator, and a carved and painted figurine known as the kachina doll. Members of the tribe, usually fathers and uncles, crafted these dolls from cottonwood roots. They added beaks, horns, feathers, shells, and turquoise, then presented their creations to children during ceremonial dances.

While other tribes recognize kachinas as part of their heritage, the Hopi have the largest assortment of the spirits, more than 250 of them. They believe that the kachinas are supernatural beings their ancestors met after emerging from the underworld, and that they lived with the people to educate them in the ways of the Hopi. The kachina takes many forms, from demon to clown. The best-known are the mudheads, comedians who entertain tribal members, visitors, and even themselves during ceremonies.

Over the years, the kachina has taken on a fourth dimension, as an art form. Hopi arti-

Kachinas:

Hand-carved from the roots of the cotton-wood tree, kachinas represent hundreds of deities sacred to the Hopi tribe.

sans carve both the older traditional dolls and newer stylistic figures, still using cottonwood root. They're sold on the Hopi Reservation, in museums, and in some authorized gift shops. Buyers should be aware that an authentic Hopi kachina is usually very expensive. Cheaper dolls are available, but they are rarely Hopi-made.

On February 14, 1912, Pres. William Howard Taft signed the official papers that made Arizona the forty-eighth, and last, state. The state held that distinction for almost 47 years.

Back in 1912, the event did not go unnoticed by those residing here. Miners in Bisbee celebrated by igniting several sticks of dynamite. The ensuing explosion almost tore the top off a nearby mountain. Folks in Snowflake were a little more reserved. They blew up an anvil. In Phoenix, plans for a forty-eight-gun salute were cut short when the reverberations from the cannon blasts shattered windows in the capitol building.

The new state didn't agree on a state flag until five years later. And when they settled on one that depicted the sun rising over a field of blue, many people protested its resemblance to the flag of Japan. Their protests were noted, but went unheeded. The flag remains the same today.

Last State:

Arizona held the designation for more than forty years.

But Arizona's reign as the last state ended in 1959, when Alaska and Hawaii were admitted to the Union. Besides being hard to pronounce, there's not much glory in being known as "the last of the forty-eight contiguous states." And "the next-to-the-next-to-the-last state" just doesn't have much dignity.

you know you're in
arizona when...
...you walk across London Bridge

The Grand Canyon is Arizona's primary tourist attraction. It has been under construction for millions of years. Holding down second place is the London Bridge, built less than 200 years ago, then torn down, moved, and reconstructed a long way from its original site. In other words, it's a transplant. But tourists don't care; millions of them flock to the shores of the Colorado River every year to either drive or walk across it.

The stone bridge was one of several London Bridges erected across the Thames River in London, beginning in A.D. 43. The first was a pontoon bridge; those that followed were made of stone. Arizona's London Bridge was completed in 1824 but was put up for auction in the mid-1960s because it was sinking into the river. About that same time, developer Robert P. McCulloch was looking for a gimmick to attract buyers to Lake Havasu City, a new town he was building on the Colorado. The bridge got his attention, and he bought it for $2.46 million and had it dismantled and shipped to Arizona, where it was put back together, stone by stone.

At first, the bridge spanned a dry piece of the Mohave Desert. But when the reconstruction was completed, the developers dug a channel that diverted part of the Colorado River to flow underneath. The total cost of the project was $7.5 million. Apparently, it was worth it. Lake Havasu City has grown into a community of 40,000 permanent residents, and an estimated two million visitors stroll across the London Bridge every year.

London Bridge:

Billed as the "world's largest antique," the bridge was taken apart in London, and then transported to the Arizona desert where it was reconstructed block by block.

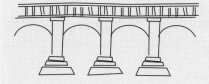

... treasure maps are an important part of the economy

From 1868 to 1886, a German immigrant named Jacob Waltz spent his winters prospecting for gold in the Superstition Mountains. He never brought much out in the spring, but when he died in 1891, forty-eight pounds of gold were found under his bed and the search was on.

Julia Thomas cared for the old miner, nicknamed "the Dutchman," in his final days and started searching the Superstitions for his Lost Dutchman Mine shortly after his death. She and her partners found nothing. Since then, a steady stream of prospectors, fortune hunters, and inquisitive speculators have plunged into the mountains searching for the lost gold. Several have died; those who survived came out empty-handed.

But legends about the lost treasure persist. Large expeditions and one-man forays have tried and met with failure. They search for gold allegedly left by the Spanish who fled in the face of Apache attacks; or gold the Apaches themselves mined, then buried; or the Dutchman's gold, which could have been either Spanish or Apache gold. (Or neither. The Dutchman was very secretive.)

In the fall of 2004, the USDA Forest Service—which controls the vast acreage covered by the Superstitions—gave rare

and unusual permission for a new expedition. The organizers hope this search will recover the cache of gold and silver bars which, they maintain, were the source of the Dutchman's gold.

But to date, the only persons who have struck it rich in this particular endeavor are the mapmakers who create the absolutely genuine, honest-to-goodness, would-we-lie-to-you Lost Dutchman Mine treasure maps that are a staple in all tourist-oriented gift shops in and around the Superstitions.

Lost Dutchman Mine:

In the late 1800s an old miner may have found gold hidden by the Spaniards or Apaches. The search for his mine goes on today.

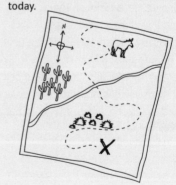

... an airfield is named after a World War I hero

A statue of Frank Luke Jr. stands in front of the Arizona State Capitol in Phoenix as a tribute to one of America's first fighter pilots who specialized in shooting down balloons. Luke graduated from high school in Phoenix, then worked in the copper mines before enlisting in the Signal Corps at the start of World War I. He was commissioned as a pilot a few months later, although many questioned why. The warplanes of that era were bulky things composed of canvas and wood and were extremely prone to crashing.

Besides that, Luke wasn't a prime example of a good war ace. He had trouble following orders and, when stationed in France, often left formation to look for enemy targets on his own. He went after German observation balloons in particular. The balloons were effective weapons because they could be stationed over enemy infantry units and direct artillery fire.

After two fellow airmen were shot down, Luke decided to go solo. On the last day of his life, although he had been grounded for disobeying orders, Luke disobeyed the order that grounded him. He took off and shot down three balloons and two enemy planes before his craft was hit by ground

Frank Luke Jr.:

A maverick pilot who specialized in balloon-bursting.

fire. Although wounded, nearly out of fuel, and about to crash, Luke swooped down and strafed a German infantry unit.

He landed in a cemetery and was quickly surrounded by Germans. He was killed shortly after he drew his pistol and started shooting. Luke became one of only two American aviators to receive the Congressional Medal of Honor in World War I. The other was Capt. Eddie Rickenbacker.

Luke Air Force Base in Glendale is named after the Phoenix hero.

John McPhee's plan was brilliant, but the details needed a little work.

McPhee was the editor of a Mesa newspaper in 1932 when he conceived a scheme to promote local merchants as well as his publication. The plan was to hire an airplane and a stuntman. They'd dress the stuntman as Santa Claus, then fly him over a designated spot where he would leap from the plane, open his parachute, drift to the ground, and distribute gifts.

But on the day of the Great Santa Jump, McPhee found Santa in a nearby saloon, building up his fortitude glass by glass. Unfortunately, the stuntman had overestimated his capacity for liquid courage and was in no shape to get on the plane, much less jump out of it.

Undaunted, McPhee located a department store mannequin and dressed it as St. Nick. He loaded the dummy onto the plane and instructed the pilot to shove it out after pulling the parachute's rip cord. The fake Santa was supposed to land behind some buildings, where McPhee would be waiting in another Santa suit. He'd take the dummy's place and distribute the goodies.

The plane circled, McPhee donned his white beard and red suit and waited, and the pilot pushed the dummy out of the airplane. But the parachute didn't open. So instead of drifting gently to the ground, Santa Claus plunged headfirst into a nearby field while hundreds of spectators watched in horror.

McPhee, however, carried on. He jumped from his hiding place and began his Santa Claus routine. But it was too late. Moms and dads hustled their stunned kiddies away from the scene and away from the stores that were supposed to benefit from the stunt.

The embarrassed McPhee left town for a while, then returned to work. But when he died in 1968, the headline over his obituary in the newspaper he once ran read: "John McPhee, the man who killed Santa Claus, dies."

John McPhee:

He became a legend when a Christmas plot went awry.

Mesquite trees are common in southern Arizona, where they've evolved to a point that they need very little water. This is an important adaptation for survival in the desert. The small leaves of mesquite trees reduce the loss of moisture through aspiration, and their tap roots can bore as deep as 100 feet in their search water.

The wood of the mesquite has an interesting pattern of whirls, swirls, and varying shades because the trees aren't straight. During their formative years, they twist, turn, and change direction so often that the wood becomes distorted. After a lifetime of that sort of activity, the grain has more zigs, zags, and swoops than a plate of overcooked spaghetti.

Also, mesquite wood suffers from voids, flaws, defects, cracks, wormholes (the insect variety, not the sci-fi type), and knots that make it practically unusable for anything functional. The imperfections also wreak havoc with saws and lathes, so many woodworkers throw mesquite away or use it as firewood.

Working with mesquite, therefore, is very labor intensive. Producing something as small as an end table can take up to three weeks. The cracks and other flaws have to be filled with a form of epoxy. Because of the diversity in the grain, it's difficult to match one piece with another. And the workers have to use extra caution during the smoothing and shaping process, or the wood will tear and split.

The idiosyncrasies may have something to do with the mesquite's birth process. Its seed pods have to pass through the digestive tracts of cattle, deer, or other browsing animals before they'll sprout. The animals' digestive juices eat away the seed coat, allowing water to penetrate the seed so the germination process can begin.

Despite the problems, there are places that manufacture mesquite furniture and sell it on a wide market. A primary example is Arroyo Designs in Tucson (520–884–1012; www.arroyo-design.com), where you can pick up something like a four-drawer chest for something like $6,000. A bit expensive, perhaps, but they have to pay for the aggravation and ruined saw blades somehow.

Mesquite:

A desert tree that can survive on humidity, the mesquite twists and turns so badly that most people use it only for firewood. Others turn it into furniture.

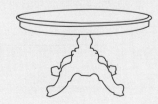

you know you're in
arizona when ...
... you have the right to remain silent

Although Ernesto Miranda was hardly what one would call a hero, or even an antihero, his name and his situation are firmly embedded in the nation's judicial system.

Miranda, a Phoenix truck driver, kidnapped and raped an eighteen-year-old girl in 1963. He was caught and immediately confessed, then was convicted and sentenced to a lengthy prison term.

But Phoenix attorneys John Flynn and John Frank appealed, saying Miranda's rights hadn't been protected after his arrest. They argued that he hadn't been told he didn't have to speak to police without a lawyer present. In 1966, they took the case all the way to the U.S. Supreme Court, which ruled in their favor, and the Miranda Rights ruling went into effect. The ruling is the one that starts, "You have the right to remain silent . . . ."

Ernest Miranda:

A petty criminal, Ernesto Miranda of Phoenix achieved some degree of fame when the Miranda law was named after him. The law says officers must inform suspects of their rights.

MIRANDA RIGHTS

YOU HAVE THE RIGHT TO
REMAIN SILENT

ANYTHING YOU SAY CAN AND
WILL BE USED AGAINST YOU
IN A COURT OF LAW

YOU HAVE THE RIGHT TO
TALK TO A LAWYER AND HAVE
HIM PRESENT WITH YOU
WHILE YOU ARE BEING
QUESTIONED

ETC.

Miranda, while granted a new trial, was convicted again and sent back to prison. He was paroled in 1973 and died in 1976 from stab wounds suffered in a barroom brawl.

you know you're in
arizona when...
...you can pronounce "Mogollon Rim"

Two things associated with the Mogollon Rim attract a great deal of attention. The first deals with its origins.

The Rim is an escarpment that defines the southwestern edge of the Colorado Plateau. It was uplifted eons ago by shifts in the earth's surface and now extends about 450 miles, crossing nearly half the state, from Sedona to the New Mexico border.

The limestone and sandstone cliffs that once marked the border of a huge inland lake were formed from sediments deposited during the Carboniferous and Permian Periods. Over the ages, erosion and faulting have carved spectacular canyons into cliffs, making the Rim a popular venue for campers, hikers, and those who like to admire the beauty of the outdoors.

The escarpment rises from 4,000 feet to more than 7,000 feet and is covered with a variety of plant and animal life. It is also the site of the largest stand of ponderosa pine on the continent.

The second item deals with pronunciation. Most newcomers and visitors (and even a few permanent residents) say it phonetically, "mo-GO-lon." Others, aware of the Hispanic influence in Arizona in which the *ll* becomes a *y*, will utter "mo-GOgo-yon."

Neither is correct. It's "MUGGY-own."

Mogollon Rim:

Ancient and beautiful, but phonetically incorrect.

you know you're in
arizona when...
...you spot a Mount Graham squirrel

There are fewer than 300 Mount Graham squirrels in the United States and they all live, naturally, on Mount Graham, a landmass that rises 10,717 feet above sea level near Safford. They resemble several other species of squirrel; their rarity is what makes them noteworthy.

A 2004 survey counted 264 of the endangered squirrels, a decline of twenty from the previous year's census. Their habitat is imperiled by an extended drought and forest fires.

The establishment of a huge telescope complex known as the Mount Graham International Observatory, along with the

Mount Graham Squirrel:

An endangered species threatened by the presence of astronomers.

support services it requires and an influx of tourists visiting the scope, further threatens the squirrels.

...Sandra Day O'Connor is one of your heroes

Even though she earned degrees in economics and law from Stanford University, and even though her husband was an attorney, Sandra Day O'Connor had difficulty finding work as lawyer. That was back in the early 1950s.

Today she is pretty well known in the field of law because she serves on the United States Supreme Court. In 1981 President Reagan appointed her to fill a vacancy left by Associate Justice Potter Stewart's retirement. The Judiciary Committee approved her by a 17–1 vote; later the U.S. Senate confirmed the appointment with a 99–0 favorable vote.

The confirmations made her the first woman ever to sit on the U.S. Supreme Court.

Sandra Day was born in El Paso, Texas, in 1930. Her family moved to a ranch near Duncan, Arizona, when she was an infant. After graduation from Stanford with her law and economics degrees, she received only one job offer: a legal secretary's position that required "excellent typing skills."

O'Connor served as a civilian lawyer for the Quartermaster Corps while her husband was in the military. When the couple moved to Phoenix, she got a part-time job in the office of the state attorney general. In 1965 she was appointed to the Arizona

Senate; later she was elected to serve a full term and eventually became the first woman to serve as the majority leader of a state senate.

In 1974 O'Connor was elected a Maricopa County trial judge. In 1979 she was appointed to the State Court of Appeals. In 1981 Reagan tapped her for her biggest job as a lawyer. She was inducted into the National Women's Hall of Fame in 1995, and has a high school named in her honor in north Phoenix. Obviously, she no longer has trouble finding a job.

Sandra Day O'Connor:

Once unable to find work, she now sits on the highest court in the land.

you know you're in
arizona when . . .

... you sing "Arrrizona, where the wind comes sweepin' down the plain ..."

Think about it: Oklahoma is where the wind comes waving through the wheat fields, and Arizona is where the dust devils go dancing through the sand. Hard to believe that one could pass for the other, right?

It did happen, but, as the saying goes, "only in the movies." In the mid-1950s, after a successful run on Broadway, Rodgers and Hammerstein's *Oklahoma!* was made into a film starring Gordon McRae and Shirley Jones as the young Sooner sweethearts.

But it wasn't filmed in Oklahoma. The moviemakers decided the rolling grasslands of southeastern Arizona looked more like Oklahoma than Oklahoma did, so they brought in their lights, cameras, and actors and set up shop near Nogales.

The resemblance is pretty close. Only the most expert of agrarians will notice that the ears of corn hanging off the stalks are wax, not the real thing.

Oklahoma:

Arizona's resemblance to Oklahoma is the thing movies are made of.

Two of the West's more notorious characters were part of Arizona's early days: Pearl Hart, who participated in America's last stagecoach robbery, and Billy the Kid, who killed his first victim in what was then Arizona Territory.

Hart, dubbed the Girl Bandit by newspapers in the territory, took part in the stagecoach holdup in 1899. Nabbed a short time later, she was tried in front of an all-male jury that found her partner guilty but declared she was innocent. An outraged judge ordered another trial on a different charge, and this time Hart was found guilty. She was sentenced to five years in Yuma Prison but was released after faking a pregnancy.

The lady pistol-packer then went on the lecture circuit, telling her audiences that she became a robber so she could get enough money to visit her ailing mother.

Billy the Kid was known as Henry McCarty and worked as a horse wrangler at Fort Grant when he began his life of crime. On August 17, 1877, he got into an altercation with F. P. "Windy" Cahill, a blacksmith. Witnesses later said Cahill was getting the best of his younger adversary, so McCarty pulled out a pistol and fired a single shot into his opponent, who died the next day.

McCarty left Arizona that same night and never returned. He moved to New Mexico, changed his name to William Bonney, and was eventually gunned down by Sheriff Pat Garrett on July 14, 1881. Despite his reputation as a cold-blooded killer with many notches on his gun, historians now believe Billy's total victim count was probably no more than six.

Outlaws:

Arizona was a sort of training ground for some notorious baddies.

you know you're in
arizona when ...
... the desert looks hand-painted

At sunset, the Painted Desert looks like the work of a paint-by-numbers artist who followed every line with great precision. The reds are carefully separated from the purples, the edges of the browns never lap over into the grays, and the lines between the pinks and the mauves are clearly defined.

Some of the hues are muted; others are brilliant. The colors stretch for miles across flatlands, then plummet into mini-gorges only to rise again on the other side. Scientifically, these are deposits of clay, sandstone, silt, stone, and hematite. Artistically, however, they are scarlets and umbers and taupes and beiges, all carefully arranged on an endless canvas.

The Painted Desert is part of the Petrified Forest National Park in northeastern Arizona. Visitors can view the splendor at their leisure at any one of six vantage points, but they should be forewarned that none of their photographs will even remotely capture the grandeur of the sights they behold.

Painted Desert:

It resembles the work of a paint-by-numbers artist.

you know you're in
arizona when...
...rustling petrified trees is criminal—and cursed

The major portion of the Petrified Forest National Park is an awesome display of what you can do with a piece of wood—if you're willing to wait around for millions of years.

The 93,520-acre park spreads across portions of two counties and contains, as the name indicates, the world's best collection of petrified wood in its natural state. Well-marked trails at the visitor center lead rock hounds through hundreds of petrified logs estimated to be 225 million years old. The area was once a vast flood plain, and the tall pine-like trees that grew there were washed into streams swollen by floodwaters. They were then covered with silt, mud, and volcanic ash. Gradually silica deposits replaced the wood tissues. When the silica crystallized into quartz, the logs became petrified.

There's petrified wood just lying around everywhere in the park. The most notable pieces weigh thousands of pounds, making them safe from pilferers who might be tempted to take home a slab and convert it into a coffee table. But millions of other pieces are little chunks that will fit easily into a pocket, so there's always a temptation to do just that.

Resist the temptation. In the first place, it's illegal to remove even the tiniest piece of the ancient wood. In the second place, those who get caught stealing face fines of up to $250. But worst of all is this: The visitor center contains a large scrapbook filled with letters written by people who stole petrified wood and then returned it because they were plagued by bad luck after committing the crime. According to their anguished writings, their punishments ranged from being attacked by stomach cramps and diarrhea to breakup with a true love to divorce.

Petrified Forest:

Millions of years ago, northern Arizona was a verdant forest land. But the climate changed; the trees died, got buried, got petrified, and then resurfaced as tourist attractions.

Although many people mistakenly think so, the roadrunner is not Arizona's official state bird. The cactus wren is; New Mexico picked the roadrunner. Despite that, the roadrunner is commonly associated with Arizona. It's probably because when the famous roadrunner in the cartoons outwitted the embattled Wile E. Coyote, the confrontations appeared to be in the Arizona desert.

Arizonans also keep the bird's notoriety alive by reciting a variety of legends about its skills, particularly the way it catches and eats rattlesnakes. Roadrunners occasionally do catch and devour rattlesnakes, but they don't actively pursue them. Since a snake is usually more than a bird can handle at one sitting, roadrunners are sometimes spotted running through the desert with half-consumed snakes hanging from their mouths. It's not an everyday scenario, but it happens.

As for the legends, one is that the birds will chance upon a sleeping snake and build a cactus corral around the reptile. When the snake awakens, the roadrunner goads it into striking and the reptile gets hopelessly entangled in the cactus and becomes an easy lunch for the bird.

Roadrunner:

An Arizona icon, this bird got most of its notoriety as Wile E. Coyote's foe in the cartoon series. But it's not the state's official bird. The cactus wren is.

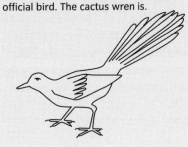

Another story is that the roadrunner picks up a cactus pod with its bill and charges a snake, which responds by lashing out and taking a bunch of spines right in the schnozzola. After a while, the snake has so many spines stuck in its face that it can't crawl away, so the roadrunner puts it out of its misery by eating it.

None of the stories are true, except for the part about roadrunners snarfing down an occasional rattler. Some skeptics even dispute the part about uneaten snakes hanging from a roadrunner's bill; hundreds of others say they've seen it themselves.

... you see shrines along the highways

Roadside shrines are common along Arizona's highways and byways, but some leave more lasting impressions because of their size, history, and construction.

The largest is Our Lady of the Sierras Shrine, off Highway 92 near Hereford. It features a 75-foot Celtic cross, a 30-foot statue of the Blessed Virgin Mary, and a chapel built with wooden beams hauled to the site from Michigan.

The Shrine of St. Joseph of the Mountains in Yarnell contains several life-size scenes from the life of Jesus Christ, all cast in concrete. The shrine, built in the 1940s, is located off Highway 89 on a hill surrounded by huge boulders.

Others are smaller but no less notable. On Highway 60 outside of Miami, Ruben Licano tends to the shrine he built to fulfill a promise he made in the 1950s. He was serving in the U.S. Army during the Korean War and vowed that if he got home safely, he'd erect a shrine to honor the Virgin Mary. His shrine is made of river rock and reinforcing rods.

North of Flagstaff, the Chapel of the Holy Dove is a familiar sight once more. Originally built in 1963, it was destroyed by fire in 1999. Local residents pitched in to restore it, and now it's open to anyone in need of quiet and reflection. Located off

Highway 180, it's also a popular spot for weddings.

A few miles north of Yuma on Highway 95, farmer Loren Pratt built Arizona's smallest church, to honor the memory of his wife. The chapel seats only six people.

The Telles family hammered out a niche in a rocky hillside on Highway 83 near Patagonia to build the shrine they promised if their sons returned home safely from World War II. Concrete steps lead to the site, now blackened by smoke from the thousands of candles lit there by the family and visitors. And their sons did survive the war.

Roadside Shrines:

The state is dotted with roadside shrines dedicated to promises made while in the military, to honor a late spouse, or for a son to come home safely from war.

you know you're in
arizona when...
... artists use rocks instead of canvas

The petroglyphs inscribed on boulders by ancient Native Americans are relatively common throughout Arizona, but there's another form of rock art that doesn't draw nearly as much interest or speculation. It's historic, sort of, but it dates back decades instead of centuries.

One example is a fifteen-ton boulder on Highway 89 near Congress, painted green and white to resemble a giant frog. The transformation occurred in the 1920s, when a young housewife and her sons got bored with staring at the desert and decided it needed some beautification.

Railroad workers with time and extra paint on their hands performed a similar conversion near Hilldale in about 1900. Using black and white paint left over from a railroad sign-painting job they had completed, they turned a huge rock into a gigantic skull. It's on Date Creek Road, 6.3 miles north of Congress.

Several granite boulders in the Cerbat Mountains near Chloride were given a makeover in the 1950s by Nevada artist

Roy Purcell. He used automobile paint to create abstract scenes that involve snakes, a woman named Animus, and a Chloride street scene. The painted rocks are 1.3 miles south of Chloride, which is 15 miles north of Kingman on Highway 93.

All of these works have withstood the elements well and are still highly visible, once you find them.

Rock Art:

Arizona artists use boulders to create their masterpieces.

you know you're in
arizona when ...
... you attend the world's oldest rodeo(s)

Many other states hold rodeos, but only Arizona can claim to be home to not only the world's oldest rodeo but to *both* of the world's oldest rodeos. They're held annually, and the dispute over which is actually the oldest was once such an issue that a truce had to be worked out.

There was a time when both Prescott and Payson laid claim to the bragging rights for hosting the "world's oldest rodeo." While there was no threat of going to war over it, citizens of both communities used to get pretty ornery when the subject came up. But the ruckus has died down to a point where now it's nothing more than a question of semantics.

Payson staged its first rodeo as a form of hometown entertainment in 1884, four years before Prescott came up with a similar idea. But Prescott started paying out prize money first, thus elevating bronco-busting and calf-roping to the higher form that evolved into the rodeo, giving that city a legitimate claim to the "world's oldest" honor.

But Prescott cancelled its rodeos for a couple of years during World War II, while Payson kept right on a-buckin' and a-ropin' and then a-claimin' that the Prescott inter-

ruption put Payson back in first place in the longevity race.

Rather than continue this sort of wrangling, the cities called a truce and settled the issue with the insertion of one word into Payson's designation. So now Prescott stages the "World's Oldest Rodeo," and Payson annually holds the "World's Oldest Continuous Rodeo."

And everybody's happy.

Except maybe those cowboys who get thrown off the backs of angry bulls.

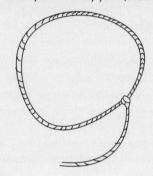

Rodeos:

Arizona is home to both of the world's oldest rodeos. This rare and unusual feat is accomplished every year. (Usually.)

you know you're in
arizona when ...
... you find a Navajo rug

According to Navajo tradition, rug weaving became a part of Navajo culture when their ancient Holy People first bestowed the concept on the Spider Woman, a Navajo deity. She then taught a young Navajo woman the art, and it has been passed on from one generation to the next. The designs are conceptualized in the mind of the weaver, and she involves herself in its creation to the point that she leaves the rug's border open at one spot. This allows the spirit of the weaver to exit when the rug is completed.

Navajo rugs are used in tribal homes and, over the past 150 years, have become collectors' items among non-Navajos. They vary in size from small rugs that can be used as coasters to others large enough to cover a living room floor. But most buyers display their rugs as wall hangings rather than let people walk on them.

For those interested in a really, really big Navajo rug, there's one at Chilchinbito that measures 38 feet by 24 feet. It is one of the largest Navajo rugs ever made. After a huge loom was erected in the gymnasium of the local school, ten women from Chilchinbito worked on the rug for two years, incorporating twenty-five designs to represent different weaving patterns. Since

Rugs:

Navajo rugs are still made by hand. They have many imitators, but authentic rugs are among the hottest items at trading posts and Indian fairs.

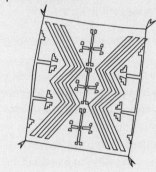

its completion in 1979, the rug has been displayed at the Navajo Nation Fair, the 1984 presidential inauguration in Washington, D.C., and in Kansas City and Phoenix.

Tribal officials said the project cost around $100,000. Offers from potential buyers, ranging from $200,000 to $5.2 million, have been rejected by the tribe, which prefers to keep the rug rolled up in the school. It is taken out of storage only for special occasions, such as high school graduations.

Although the saguaro cactus is indigenous only to the Sonoran Desert, it has become symbolic of all deserts in the Southwest. Since this species is common in Arizona, there's a ready association between the saguaro and the state. The saguaro blossom is Arizona's official state flower.

Saguaros don't grow very fast. They begin life as tender seedlings, standing only a quarter of an inch high after two years. They may be only 4 to 6 inches high after ten years; they don't produce their first blooms until sometime between their thirtieth and fortieth years, when they may still be a mere 10 feet tall; and they don't develop branches until sometime after their seventieth year.

Eventually, however, the giants of the desert can reach heights of 50 feet and weigh up to ten tons. At one time, an armless saguaro near Cave Creek measured an estimated 72 feet tall, but it fell over during a wind storm not long after that.

The saguaro's water absorption mechanism is an engineering marvel. Its root system can have a radius of 30 to 50 feet. After a rainfall the roots transport hundreds of gallons of water up into the trunk, where the pulpy storage tissue expands like an accordion. Thus gorged, a veteran saguaro can weigh up to 20,000 pounds, 90 percent of it water.

The state's current record holder stands near Horseshoe Lake northeast of Scottsdale. It's just under 50 feet tall, has fifteen arms, measures 94 inches in diameter at the base, and is on the National Register of Big Trees, a list maintained by the conservation group American Forests. Another old-timer located near Quartzsite isn't all that tall, but it does have forty-six arms, which may not be a record but is well above average.

The plants are honored and protected in the Saguaro National Park near Tucson.

Saguaro:

Arizona's most endearing symbol can grow to more than 50 feet and weigh as much as 20,000 pounds.

you know you're in
arizona when...
...salsa warms your gizzard

Salsa is a popular condiment usually associated with, but not confined to, Mexican food. The combination of tomatoes, peppers, and onions comes in several varieties. These include Wimp Salsa, which registers a mere burp on the salsa meter; Heartburn Hotel, always served with Pepto Bismol; and Richter Scale Salsa, often blamed for the San Francisco earthquake of 1906.

Salsa cooking contests are open to anyone, even those who know nothing about making the stuff. This results in salsas called Attack of the Fire-Breathing Tomatoes; Big Bad Belchbelly; Widowmaker; Fire Down Below; and Your Hearse or Mine.

Those who attend salsa cook-offs should make pre-dining preparations. Among them:

- Choose salsa-eating clothing with care, as any salsa worthy of the name can melt polyester.
- Avoid salsa served by a person wearing a welder's mask and asbestos gloves.
- Don't trust any salsa that tries to conceal its b.p.m. (belches per minute) with a friendly name, such as Aloha Salsa. All that means is that the cook used molten lava instead of chili peppers.
- Remember that salsa is not governed by any international agency, so it doesn't have to take prisoners.

Some salsas don't turn your stomach into a boiling cauldron of agony. Here's the recipe for one kinder and gentler type:

10 Roma tomatoes
6 cloves garlic, peeled and chopped
1 white onion, peeled and chopped
1 small jalapeño pepper, chopped
2 larger jalapeño peppers, chopped
½ cup fresh cilantro, chopped
1 bunch green onions, trimmed and
    chopped
8-ounce can tomato sauce

Chop tomatoes (do not use food processor), then mix all ingredients together in medium-size, nonreactive bowl. Add enough cold water to suit. Let stand for four hours in the refrigerator before eating.

Salsa:

Arizona's answer to catsup, mustard, and pickle relish. Goes on everything, goes well with everything.

The Parada del Sol, held every year in Scottsdale, is billed as "the world's largest horse-drawn parade." An average of 160 entries march up Scottsdale Road in early February, and the ranks include horse-drawn buggies and carriages, marching bands, drill teams, and lone riders.

The parade marks the opening of the annual Parada del Sol Rodeo, a two-day event where people pay money to see how fast a cowboy can fall off a bull.

To the south, the Tucson Rodeo starts every year with "the world's largest non-motorized parade," which differs from the world's largest horse-drawn parade only slightly. The parade and rodeo are held annually in late February, and the parade is so popular that children are let out of school to watch it.

Humans who march in either or both rodeo parades require a talent unique to horse-related events. Because the horses are not parade-broken, so to speak, they frequently make large deposits along the parade

Scoopers:

Skilled shovel wielders who keep parade routes safe for tuba players.

route. As a result, baton twirlers must be adept at watching where they step while maintaining a close watch on their flying batons.

The parades also provide temporary employment for groups known as "used hay and oats collectors," more commonly referred to as "pooper scoopers." They're usually service club members or teenagers armed with shovels and buckets who are trying to pick up, as it were, a little money for charity.

you know you're in
arizona when...
...Sedona's vortex beckons

A relatively small community of about 17,000 solace-seekers, Sedona is one of the state's top five tourist attractions, primarily because of the sculptures Nature has carved out of the red sandstone cliffs that surround it.

Eons of erosion have shaped some of the cliffs into semi-recognizable forms that, thanks to people's tendencies to name things because of their resemblance to other things, bear such designations as Snoopy Rock, Teapot Rock, and Bell Rock. They look down on an estimated four million visitors every year, most of them armed with sketch pads or the latest photographic equipment.

Sedona was named after Sedona Schnebly, wife of pioneer Theodore Carl Schnebly. He originally wanted to name his town Schnebly Station or Oak Creek Crossing but when the U.S. Post Office declared both names too long, he settled on Sedona.

Besides the lovers of sandstone figures, the city also attracts a wide variety of artists. One is Robert Shields, half of the Shields and Yarnell duo that became widely known in the 1970s for their political satire.

New Age followers also flock to Sedona because they believe there are concentrations of strong spiritual energies called vortexes emanating from the red rocks. More than a dozen vortex-related businesses now cater to their needs by offering vortex expeditions, vortex literature, vortex readings, vortex interpretations, and even vortex-inspired muscle-relaxing therapy, all at the going vortex rates.

Sedona:

The City in the Red Rocks is among the state's top five tourist attractions.

... shrimp grow in the sand

Jumbo shrimp is an oxymoron. *Desert shrimp* would be something else, like a mirage. But shrimp do grow in the Sonoran Desert.

Shrimp farming in the state started in the mid-1990s, when Gary Wood bought a few acres of sandy wasteland near Gila Bend and scraped away enough dirt to create some ponds. He filled the ponds with water, then dumped in thousands of shrimplings (purchased from hatcheries outside the state) and called the operation Desert Sweet Shrimp.

There are now four shrimp-growing establishments in Arizona. Wood's outfit is the largest, with twenty-five ponds ranging in size from one to two acres each. Their primary markets are Asian restaurants that specialize in live seafood and gourmet outlets that don't cater to frozen items.

After the shrimp are harvested each October, the water is drained and reused as fertilizer for other crops or to raise other seafood.

Shrimp:

Although it's hot and dry, Arizona is also a hotbed of shrimp farming. The growers carve out breeding ponds in the desert and fill them with irrigation water and baby shrimps, which grow into big shrimps.

And the process provides a new answer to this oft-asked question:

Q: Whatcha dune?

A: Raising scampi.

you know you're in
arizona when ...
... cowboys can sing

Bob Nolan, Marty Robbins, and Rex Allen all grew up in Arizona and eventually became cowboy singing legends. But only Allen was a true cowboy. Born on a ranch, he punched cattle and learned to sing and play the guitar to help his dad, who played for Saturday night hoedowns.

After winning some talent shows for his singing, Allen left his hometown of Willcox and headed east to pursue a career as a performer. Fame didn't come easily. At one particularly low point, Allen said later, he would have returned home if he'd had enough money for a bus ticket.

Luckily, his vocal talents eventually attracted attention and he hooked up with a Chicago radio station. His next stop was Hollywood; he was the last of the singing cowboys in several B westerns. When that genre faded in the early 1950s, Allen moved on to television and starred in his own series, *Frontier Doctor*.

Bob Nolan's athletic abilities at a Tucson high school drew college scholarship offers, but his love for music and the Old West were stronger. In 1927, he boarded a freight train for California. Two years later he teamed with Leonard Slye, and they formed a singing group called the Rocky Mountaineers. Slye later became known as Roy Rogers; the Mountaineers, with the help of Tim Spenser and Hugh and Karl Farr, evolved into the Sons of the Pioneers.

When Rogers became a major film star, Nolan and the Sons were featured as cowboys in many of his movies. But Nolan also wrote western songs, including the western classics "Cool Water" and "Tumbling Tumbleweeds."

Marty Robbins took up singing while still a high school student in Glendale. By the mid-1950s he was one of the top country and western singers, and his recording of "El Paso" became the first C & W song to win a Grammy Award.

All three are now singing around That Big Campfire Up in the Sky.

Singing Cowboys:

Bob Nolan, Rex Allen, and Marty Robbins were all Arizonans.

I'LL keep ROLLING ALONG DEEP IN MY HEART IS A SONG HERE ON THE RANGE I BELONG DRIFTING ALONG WITH THE TUMBLING TUMBLEWEEDS.

you know you're in
arizona when ...
... saguaros never outlive their usefulness

The basic support system for the giant saguaro cactus is a series of woody ribs that extend from top to bottom of the main trunk and into the arms as they form. When the cactus dies, the pulpy outer material rots away and leaves the skeleton standing as sort of a natural monument.

Removing the skeletons from public land is against the law in Arizona, but it's all right to take them from privately owned areas. Once removed, they are converted into a variety of uses, all beneficial in one way or another.

For centuries, Native Americans have been adapting the ribs to help them gather food. They attach a forklike device to the end of a rib and use the tool to knock off the fruit from a living saguaro. The ribs have also been converted into roofing material.

Landscape architects use the entire cactus skeleton when designing desert landscaping, and woodworkers carve human and animal faces into the wood from the saguaro joints.

Professional and amateur artists in the state convert the ribs into walking sticks with intricately carved knobs on the top end. Several Arizona museums feature

Skeletons:

Old saguaros never die; they just become something else.

exhibits of furniture made from saguaro skeletons. The displays include everything from sofas to bedroom chests. Cactus furniture never made it big in the home furnishing industry, but there was enough of it around so that it wasn't a rarity in the days before plywood and veneer overtook the market place.

Although they're feared by most and are often cast as dreaded foes in horror movies, rattlesnakes can actually be useful as merchandise and marketing devices.

The Steak House and Saloon at Rawhide, an Old West tourist town in Scottsdale, serves rattlesnake meat as an appetizer—or, for those who can't get enough, as an entree. Those who partake get a certificate attesting to their gastronomical fortitude.

Out in the desert near Tombstone, John and Sandy Weber operate Rattlesnake Crafts, an enterprise that turns rattlers into jewelry and accessories. The reptilian entrepreneurs have state licenses to hunt limited numbers of the snakes. Once properly dispatched, every part of the snake is used. The vertebrae and fangs are converted into necklaces and earrings; the skin is used to make belts; and the severed heads adorn the front of baseball caps.

And, of course, rattlesnakes are big in sports. In baseball, the Arizona Diamondbacks play in the National League West, and the Tucson Sidewinders, a

Snakes:

Rattlers, sidewinders, diamondbacks: The venomous snakes are protected by the state and venerated as athletic teams in Arizona.

Diamondbacks farm club, compete in the Pacific Coast League. The state's entry in the Arena Football League is the Arizona Rattlers.

There are eleven distinct species of rattlesnakes residing within Arizona's boundaries. Many of them are protected by the state's Game and Fish Department.

... the snowbirds migrate

I In politically correct terms, they're *winter visitors,* but most Arizonans call them snowbirds. They start arriving in late autumn, spend the winter, then depart in the spring. They follow the same migratory routes every year as they flee the wintry blasts of Kensal, North Dakota; Vancouver, British Columbia; International Falls, Minnesota; Chicago, Illinois; and Bangor, Maine, for the welcoming sunshine of southern Arizona, where winter daytime temperatures rarely drop below sixty degrees.

Once in Arizona, they congregate in large flocks at snowbird refuges in Mesa, Apache Junction, Casa Grande, Quartzsite, and Yuma. They nestle in large mobile habitats known as Winnebagos or fifth wheels, often brightly decorated with symbols of other places they have landed.

Although most consider them harmless and welcome them with open arms and cash registers, snowbirds are often prey for newspaper columnists, editorial cartoonists, and some Arizona drivers who consider them a menace because they clog up the roadways.

Snowbirds:

Snowy-haired folk who migrate to Arizona in the winter and leave a lot of money behind when they depart in the spring.

Despite that, they are a valuable source of income for the state. The Arizona Center for Business Research at Arizona State University estimates that nearly 300,000 snowbirds descend upon the state every year, and when the season ends, they have left more than $500 million of their money behind.

you know you're in
arizona when . . .
. . . you make son-of-a-gun stew

Every cook on the range has his own recipe for son-of-a-gun stew. Supermarkets and convenience stores aren't always nearby during a cattle drive, so cooks make do with what they have. This often includes surprise ingredients, unknown elements that frequently produce inquiries and responses such as "You don't want to know"; "Eat it, it's good for you"; and the infamous "If you lived in China, you'd eat that without being so persnickety." The stew dates back to the 1800s, when cattle roundups were much more frequent than they are now; it remains a favorite at cook-outs (both dude and genuine) today.

For those who want some real Old West flavor, here's one original recipe from *Beans 'N' Things,* written by Winkie Crigler of Eagar, Arizona. Remember that substitutions are allowed in the name of political correctness and stomach preference. (Also remember that camp cooks are at a premium so nobody should argue with them. If the camp cook gets in a huff and quits, the campers have to survive on grub worms or, even worse, the broken potato chips and cheese puffs they find behind the seats in their SUVs.)

Son-of-a-gun Stew:

A favorite concoction of cowboys a century ago, still a favorite with campers today, but with some alterations.

2 pounds lean meat
½ heart
1½ pounds liver
1 set brains
1 set sweetbreads
tripe
salt, pepper, suet, and hot sauce to taste

Dice all ingredients into bite-size pieces. Dust in some flour. Render suet in Dutch oven and use to brown ingredients. When browned, add enough water to cover and simmer for several hours, stirring occasionally. Then eat it. And you'd better like it or else.

you know you're in
arizona when...
...Spider Rock casts her shadow

Spider Rock juts out of the floor of Canyon de Chelly and rises more than 800 feet, almost to the top of the surrounding rim near Chinle on the Navajo Reservation. The canyon itself is one of Nature's better creations, carved into the arid landscape by wind and water to expose the brilliant red sandstone cliffs that form the walls. Even more impressive, several monoliths have withstood the pressures of wind, rain, cold, sun, and heat, and they stand in the middle of the canyon in defiance to the elements. Of these, Spider Rock is the most magnificent of the magnificent. Tall and slender, it resembles a rough-hewn obelisk placed to show the way to hidden treasure or, perhaps, the gravesite of an immortal.

The legend that surrounds Spider Rock is equally interesting. According to the Navajo creation story, the spire is named for the Spider Woman, a Navajo deity whose main job appears to be that of child disciplinarian. The legend says that after the Spider Woman chose the top of the rock as her home, some of the rocks at the very top turned white. The scientific explanation is that the sun bleached the rocks. But the more colorful legend, one that some parents like to tell their unruly offspring, is that the white rocks are the bones of bad children. When the Spider Woman hears of a child's misdeeds from Speaker Rock (a nearby 650-foot spire), she swoops down, grabs the errant child, and flies back to the top of the rock, where the youngster is devoured and the bones added to the white pile.

Visitors who want to enter the canyon for a close-up look at the two spires must make arrangements with Navajo guide outfits. For information, call (928) 810–8505 or log on to www.DiscoverNavajo.com. However, both the sandstone formations are quite visible from the South Rim drive that overlooks the canyon. The view from the top of the rim also affords the best photo opportunities because the rocks are too big to photograph from the bottom.

Spider Rock:

Deep within Canyon de Chelly, Spider Rock rises almost 900 feet above the floor of the canyon and provides a home for the Spider Woman, who punishes bad children.

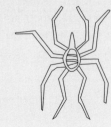

The folks who populate Winslow don't let adversity stand in the way of a good project. When they proposed a park to honor a single verse in a song, state officials ridiculed them. One even said they'd be the "laughing stock of Arizona" if they went ahead with the idea. They built it anyway. And now thousands of tourists get off Interstate 40 at Winslow every year to stand on an immortalized corner.

The song was "Take It Easy," a big hit recorded by The Eagles in the 1980s. The verse in question tells about a young man standing on a corner in Winslow, Arizona. A girl drives by in a flatbed Ford, and she slows down to check him out.

The recording became so popular that music lovers from all over the nation started getting off Interstate 40 at Winslow and driving in to town to stand on a corner. Trouble was, nobody knew for sure which corner to stand on. Realizing that this was a matter of nationwide concern, the citizens of Winslow converted a small plot of ground into the Standin' on the Corner in Winslow Arizona Park.

It's not very big, but it's large enough to accommodate the corner-standers who make the detour and leave their vehicles to get their pictures taken with the park's centerpiece, a life-size bronze statue of a young man and his guitar.

Life hasn't been all that easy for the young man, however. The rear of his pants is getting shiny, as women of all ages seem fond of rubbing his behind as they pose for the photographs.

The park is on the corner of Kimsey Avenue and Second Street in downtown Winslow. Go. Stand. Smile. Rub. It's free.

Standin':

The townspeople of Winslow figured music lovers needed a corner to stand on, so they built one.

you know you're in
arizona when...
...tourists find Mr. Wright

Master architect Frank Lloyd Wright built Taliesin West as a personal residence and an architectural school in the desert north of Scottsdale. The original Taliesin (a Welsh name for "Shining Brow") is in Spring Green, Wisconsin, but Wright became enamored of the Sonoran Desert, so he moved part of his operation here in 1937.

Years after Wright's death it's still a school, but it has also become a tourist attraction that draws nearly 125,000 visitors a year. His personal rooms feature skylights and rustic redwood beams combined with rock-and-mortar walls that sheltered Wright and his priceless book and art collections.

Of particular interest is the bedroom where the architect took daily naps on cots that seem totally out of place next to the pricey Japanese screens that served as room dividers. According to those who knew him, the room was his sanctuary. "When Wright went into his bedroom, unless the

Taliesen West:

Designed and built by architect Frank Lloyd Wright, this stone-and-concrete complex now serves as a school for architects and as a tourist attraction.

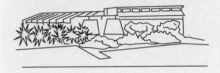

world was coming to an end, you left him alone," said architect Arnold Roy, a manager for the Frank Lloyd Wright Foundation.

Wright's legacy also lives on in north Scottsdale, where a large spire he designed in the 1930s has been erected at the corner of Scottdale Road and Frank Lloyd Wright Boulevard.

you know you're in
arizona when...
...tamale pie is a regular at mealtime

Tamale pie has three things working in its favor: It goes well with everything, it can be served at any of the three daily meals, and it'll taste good regardless of who makes it.

The pie isn't really a pie in the traditional sense of the word. That is, you shouldn't load it up with vanilla ice cream and call it "tamale pie a la mode." But as an entree, it satisfies most appetites, especially for those diners who like some zing with their victuals.

There are countless recipes for tamale pie and each recipe has more than likely undergone some tweaking. But the basic ingredients are usually the same—red or green corn tamales, salsa, cheese, and chips. While many novice cooks tend to overspice their creations so much that they taste like liquid barbed wire, veteran tamale pie-makers go for a more subtle approach that satisfies the hunger without superficially wounding it.

Here's one well-respected recipe that has tamed many an ornery case of the "hongries."

6 cooked green corn tamales
12 ounces salsa
½ cup shredded Mexican blend or
    Monterey Jack cheese
¼ cup sour cream
¼ cup crushed tortilla chips

Heat oven to 400 degrees. Spray 10-inch pan with cooking spray. Line pan with crust (store-bought works just fine). Unwrap tamales from husks and paper; crumble and press into bottom of pan. Top with all other ingredients and bake for thirty minutes. Let it stand for about fifteen minutes, then slice. Serves four.

Tamale Pie:

A delicacy made of tamales, cheese, and anything else that fits.

you know you're in
arizona when...
...tarantulas share your space

Tarantulas get a bad rap both in movies and in real life. In both scenarios, they are often depicted as rampaging monsters bent on snarfing down as many humans as possible. They make good movie monsters because they have eight long, hairy legs and eight beady little eyes. But tarantulas are not nearly as ferocious as they look.

In fact, despite what the movies say, there is no record of a human ever dying from a tarantula bite. These arachnids are generally mild creatures that can easily be tamed as house pets, and they eat insects, not people. The tarantula kills with bites from its venomous fangs. Once the victim expires, it is ground into a little ball and covered with digestive fluids. The tarantula sucks up the liquefied lunch or wraps it in a cocoon for a later snack. It is small wonder, then, that tarantulas are never invited to formal dinner parties.

There are more than 800 species of tarantulas worldwide; those found in Arizona are known as desert tarantulas, and their average leg span is 3 to 5 inches. Protected by a hairy covering that is prickly to the touch, the creatures go through life fairly unmolested and can live up to thirty years.

Tarantulas:

They're big, hairy, and scary, but not really all that bad.

Their only real enemies, besides the heroes who knock off the 40-footers in the science fiction movies, are wasps known as tarantula hawks. The wasps immobilize tarantulas, then drag them into tunnels where they lay eggs on their victims' bodies. When the eggs hatch, the larvae emerge and dine on the tarantula.

It's sort of a "what goes around, comes around" scenario.

Percival Lowell had been around the world, served his country as a statesman, written books, counted the stars, and studied mathematics before he arrived in Flagstaff in 1894. But his true love was astronomy, and he came here to establish an observatory where he could study the night skies without interference from the artificial lights of a city.

By 1902 Lowell became convinced that there was an undiscovered planet out there, somewhere beyond Neptune. Using his math skills and large telescopes, he tracked irregularities in the motions of stars in Neptune's orbit, then calculated where the new planet should be. But Lowell never actually observed the planet himself, and after his death in 1916, his work languished at the observatory for almost fourteen years.

Then in February of 1930, astronomer Clyde Tombaugh found the planet right where Lowell had said it would be. Tombaugh, who had worked with Lowell at the observatory, used his mentor's calculations and a large telescope specially designed for the quest to make the find.

This was the first time a planet had been discovered in an American observatory.

The staff at Lowell called it Pluto at the suggestion of a schoolgirl who thought it would be nice to name something after the mythical god of the underworld. But observatory staffers also noted that the first two letters of Pluto were also Percival Lowell's initials.

The Lowell Observatory still searches the night skies with much of the same equipment its founder used.

Telescopes:

Arizona is home to some of the world's largest telescopes, including those at Kitt Peak, Mount Graham, and the Lowell Observatory, where Pluto was discovered.

To most tourists, few towns capture the flavor of the Old West like Tombstone, Arizona. But the credit for much of the image is mistakenly attributed to an infamous gunfight, rather than the hardscrabble miners who wouldn't give up.

Tombstone was the site of the gunfight at the O.K. Corral, a brief moment in history that has enamored Hollywood and Old West enthusiasts ever since it occurred in 1881. But before that, and for quite a while afterward, it was a tough little community that kept coming back from the edge of disaster to try again.

Tombstone got off to a shaky start in early 1877, when prospector Ed Schieffelin told friends where he was headed in his efforts to strike it rich. They responded that instead of gold or silver, all he'd find were Apache warriors, rattlesnakes, and his own tombstone. But, like those who followed, Schieffelin stuck it out, and eventually his Lucky Cuss mine became one of Arizona's best silver producers. The town had about 10,000 residents by 1884, as well as legalized gambling and prostitution, gunfights, lynchings, fires, and floods.

A cigar-smoking bartender allegedly started the first, and worst, fire when his stogie ignited fumes from a barrel of whiskey. Two more fires in less than three years also did considerable damage, but the town rebuilt and persisted. And the unsanctioned hangings and gunfights provided the grave diggers at Boot Hill with steady employment.

Then the mines flooded during excessive rains from 1886 to 1887, and that just about killed the town too tough to die. The flooding closed the mines and ruined the town's economy. Without money to spend in the gambling halls, saloons, and brothels, most of the miners left.

Tombstone limped along, living on its reputation until the 1950s, when mining in a different form returned to save the town. The silver mines remained shut, but new cash came from the wallets of thousands of tourists who flocked to Tombstone to watch gunfight reenactments, tour the old mines, and peer into the cribs where the fallen doves once plied their trade.

Tombstone:

Once labeled "the town too tough to die," the city grew up around the silver mining industry. Today it mines the pockets of tourists who come to see the Old West.

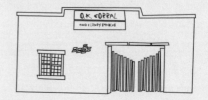

you know you're in
arizona when...
... town names are tongue twisters

Although English is the official language, Hispanic and Native American influences are evident throughout Arizona, particularly in place names, words, and everyday phraseology.

The state's name probably comes from a Spanish corruption of Indian words that was later corrupted by Anglos into its present form. A number of communities bear Spanish names— Agua Caliente (hot water), Aguila (eagle), Bonita (pretty), Canyon Diablo (devil's canyon), Casa Grande (big house), Dos Cabezas (two heads), Oro Blanco (white gold), Palo Verde (green tree), and Sierra Vista (view of the mountains), to mention a few.

Other Spanish names lead to the suspicion that somebody was messing around with the two languages just for fun. Picacho Peak, for example, is a redundancy because *picacho* is Spanish for *peak*. Also, Ajo and Nogales are both towns in Arizona. *Ajo* is Spanish for a type of garlic, and *nogales* means *walnut*.

The Mogollon Rim and Tonto National Forest are well-known areas in the state, but in some Spanish translations, *mogollon* means *parasite* and *tonto* is *fool*.

Arizona cowboys rely on such words as *buckaroo, roundup,* and *lariat,* which are anglicized versions of the Spanish words *vaquero, rodeo,* and *la reata.*

And they eat *chimichangas* (little monkeys), drink *cerveza* (beer), call each other *amigo* (friend), and answer *sí* (yes) when asked if they'd like *un otra cerveza* ('nother one).

Many of the most uncommon names found in the state are on the Indian reservations—names like Gu Vo, Ak Chut Voya, Klagetoh, and Nazlini.

And Bidahochi, Cababi, Halvana Nakya, Pisinimo, and Polacca. Plus Cascabel, Chilchinbito, Sasabe and Seba Dalkai; Tees Noh, Teec Nos Pos, and Tees Nez lah; and Shungopavi, Topowah, Vaya Chin, and Tumacacori.

Repeat all of them aloud fifteen times without stopping and you shouldn't have any more trouble with "rubber baby buggy bumpers."

Town Names:

Many Arizona towns and phrases have Hispanic and Native American backgrounds.

Tsegi, Tsaile, comoBABi, BoBoquivARi, Kots Kug AnP Kupk, LuKAchuKAi, MoenKopi, Kyotsmovi AnP Quijotos

you know you're in
arizona when ...
... your Christmas tree is a weed

Tumbleweeds sprang from noble beginnings, but today they're pests that serve no useful purpose. The ancestors of some varieties were imported from Europe as cattle feed but they got out of hand, spread across the country, and are considered pretty much worthless.

But in Chandler, tumbleweeds help to make the winter holiday season bright. Since 1957 the city has scoured the countryside for stray tumbleweeds, which are used to create a giant tree in the town center. The weeds are gently placed on a 40-foot cone made of chicken wire. Together they create the Chandler Tumbleweed Tree, the only one of its kind in the Southwest.

Once the weeds are all in place, the tree is sprayed with twenty-five gallons of white paint and fifty-five gallons of flame retardant, then adorned with fifty gallons of silver glitter and more than 1,000 lights. The mayor presides over the annual tree-lighting ceremony, and the Chandler Parks Development and Operations Division, which puts up the tree, waits for early January when it has to be removed.

Tumbleweeds:

They grow in deserts, on prairies, in cities and towns, anywhere there's open space to put down roots. Worthless except in Chandler, where they're used to make Christmas trees.

Although the tradition is almost a half-century old, its days may be numbered. Housing and business development in the area are drastically reducing the fields where the tumbleweeds once grew freely, if unwanted.

you know you're in
arizona when ...
... everyone's wearing Turquoise

Turquoise jewelry has long been associated with Navajo artisans who incorporate the gemstone into intricately fashioned earrings, necklaces, belts, and bracelets.

Considered the most valuable nontransparent mineral in the jewelry trade, turquoise has been mined since 6000 B.C., when early Egyptians began using it to adorn both the living and the dead. The name comes from a French word meaning "star of Turkey," probably because the finest turquoise is found in the Middle East.

The stone's technical name is hydrated copper aluminum phosphate, but nobody uses that, primarily because it's too long to fit on a ring. In geological circles, turquoise is considered a secondary mineral deposited from circulating waters, occurring exclusively in desert and arid environments. That explains why most of the turquoise found in the United States is unearthed in Arizona, New Mexico, and California.

Because of the big demand for turquoise, it's inevitable that fakes sometimes show up on the market. Such minerals as howlite and chrysocolla are often dyed to imitate

Turquoise:

The most valuable of the nontransparent gemstones is highly prized in Navajo jewelry.

the real thing, and some mass-marketers use inferior stones with colors stabilized by resin.

The Navajo jewelry-makers exhibit magnificent patience as they spend countless hours hammering silver into the shapes required to fit the gemstones. Many of their pieces end up in museums, but most are displayed on the necks, ears, wrists, and fingers of appreciative patrons who value the skills involved in their creation.

And some will be safely tucked away in a box in the attic until it's time to make an appearance on *Antiques Roadshow.*

you know you're in
arizona when...
... you might own a Ladmo Bag

In 1954 KPHO-TV in Phoenix began airing a local kids' program called *It's Wallace?* Over the years, the show expanded, added characters, and changed names. By 1970 it had evolved into *The Wallace and Ladmo Show,* and it ran uninterrupted until December 29, 1989, never deviating from its original format of cartoons, kiddie games, and silliness.

That thirty-five-year tenure makes it the longest-running locally produced television show in history. But even after the final show and the death of one of its leading characters, it lives on through reruns and a permanent exhibit in the Arizona State Historical Museum.

The show's stars were Bill Thompson (Wallace), the late Ladimir Kwiatkowski (Ladmo), and Pat McMahon, who played a variety of other characters. The show was often filmed before a live audience composed of youngsters. Many of the children were given Ladmo Bags, one of the most sought-after treasures of the time. These were plain brown paper sacks printed with the words *Ladmo Bag* and containing such monumental goodies as candy, trinkets, and merchandise coupons.

Most of the thousands who received the bags devoured the candy, pocketed the toys, and threw the rest away. Today, many wish they'd had a little more foresight, and they express their regret on a Web site dedicated to the show (www.wallaceand ladmo.com). The few who saved their bags have what are considered the Holy Grail of Wallace and Ladmo fans.

Those who can't live without a Ladmo Bag should be aware that even if they do find one, the candy will be almost twenty years old.

The Wallace and Ladmo Show:

A popular, locally produced kiddie TV show on the air for thirty-five years.

you know you're in
arizona when ...
... water has rights

Arizona's history as a naval power is relatively brief. It involved only two boats and zero skirmishes.

Back in the early 1930s, Arizona and California were in a state of verbal warfare over water rights from the Colorado River. Arizona maintained that California was taking more than its allotted share from the river, and things got so heated that Arizona governor Ben Moeur dispatched the National Guard to Parker and ordered them to set up machine guns along the shoreline to stop water pilferage.

The show of force, small though it was, intimidated construction workers at the Parker Dam so much that they walked off the job. Then one night during the standoff, some of the Guardsmen borrowed two steamboats to scout the waters. Since the boats were the property of local merchant Nellie Bush, the Guardsmen commissioned her as an admiral in the Arizona Navy.

There wasn't a happy ending, however. The steamboats got snarled on some cables in the river and were pulled to shore by a crew of Californians. A few days later, the Arizona Supreme Court ordered Governor Moeur to withdraw his forces, and the incident was over.

But more than seventy years later, Arizona and California are still battling over water rights from the Colorado.

Water Rights:

An ongoing dispute between Arizona and California over Colorado River water once erupted into naval warfare.

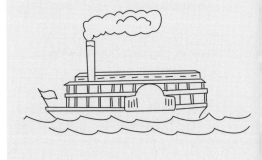

...you belly up to the bar along Whiskey Row

There are, of course, cowboy bars in several Arizona communities, but the most famous (or infamous) are those along Whiskey Row in Prescott. One of them, the Palace Saloon, is a favorite of both locals and out-of-towners because it has maintained its stature as a watering hole through hard times and the changing habits of spirits consumers.

The Palace is located toward the middle of Whiskey Row, a block-long district that once had a solid row of bars butted up against each other. Many of the originals are gone or have been converted into such nonalcoholic outlets as an ice cream store, art gallery, and sandwich shop. Others are now wine bars or other liquor dispensaries that appeal to a younger generation. But the Palace survives, still using the same wooden bar that was hauled out of the building during a fire in 1900. (The entire block burned to the ground while Palace patrons continued drinking at the bar they had rescued.)

Whiskey Row:

Back when Prescott was rip-roarin', an entire block was covered with saloons. Many of them are gone, but their stories—and some of the originals—still thrive.

Whiskey Row was unofficially established along Montezuma Street in the 1860s when the townspeople got tired of hauling drunks out of Granite Creek. The first bar to locate there was the Quartz Rock Saloon; others soon followed, and folks still find it a primary locale for the time-honored practice of the wetting of the whistle.

Racing fans in Arizona don't limit themselves to fast-moving horses, cars, boats, and greyhounds to get their kicks.

We begin with the worm races. They're held every July in the White Mountain community of Alpine. The worms are placed on a large wooden rectangle and ordered to crawl fast or become fish bait. The worm that crawls the farthest in the designated time period is the winner. Alpine also hosts dog sled races every winter.

Stock tank racing is a highlight during Cave Creek's annual Wild West Days celebration. Since stock tanks are getting scarce as housing developments take over ranch land, the rules have been expanded to allow bathtubs. The containers are welded onto steel frames with wheels. One contestant sits in the tank or tub; his or her partner uses fancy footwork to propel it from behind.

The annual Toys for Tots Bed Race in Flagstaff doesn't involve kneeling down to say your prayers or putting on your jammies. It's a sporting event in which bed-pushing athletes go bed-to-bed against each other over a course through city streets. Each team of four pushers and one rider must maneuver a course while not only steering the bed but also participating in such diversions as a belly-to-belly football tote.

Chandler holds two races every year—one for big birds, the other for small dogs. The birds are the featured runners in early March during the city's annual Ostrich Festival, an event that honors Arizona's ostrich-related heritage. (Arizona was once a hotbed of ostrich breeding when designers used their feathers to make fashion statements. Now, grown men ride the birds either bareback or in special ostrich surreys.

The city also sponsors Chihuahua races during its annual Cinco de Mayo festivities. The little dogs are turned loose on a grueling 10.7-meter course for the honor of being named king or queen of the celebration, at which time the winner gets to wear a sombrero and gloat.

And now for something a little different: cotton bale racing. This emerging competition is part of Coolidge Cotton Days. Contestants are assigned to cotton bales that weigh up to 550 pounds, and are instructed to roll them to the finish line. Anyone who has ever tried to maneuver a refrigerator across a plowed field can relate.

Worm Races:

One of the many diversions for Arizona racetrack fans looking to place a bet.

you know you're in
arizona when ...
... you yell "yee haw!"

Basically a cowboy term that supposedly originated among ranch hands in charge of breaking horses, "yee haw" is now common among folks who want to give emphasis to special occasions—such as river rafters when they hit the white water. As in "That chunk of water's going to tear your hair off! Yee haw!"

People who accidentally hunker down on a prickly pear cactus are also fond of the expression and it has worked its way into stock car racing as well. ("Looka' the way Billy Joe took that far turn on one wheel! Yee haw!")

Although it retains its greatest popularity among cowboys, "yee haw" is also a favorite among those who drink tequila straight from the bottle.

Yee Haw:

A cowboy term used when getting on a horse, falling off a horse, drinking tequila right from the bottle, sitting on a prickly pear cactus, and other inspirational activities.

you know you're in
arizona when...
...you say "yet a hey"

There are several reasons that a common Navajo phrase would be considered unusual. One is that most people don't know how to spell it. Another is that they don't know how to pronounce it. Yet another is that they say it anyway.

The phrase in question is a traditional Navajo greeting, sort of like "aloha" because it's used as both "hello" and "goodbye." When spoken by a Navajo, it sounds like "yah ah tay" or "yeh eh tey," but it's not spelled like that. Anglos tend to simplify both pronunciation and spelling by spelling it "yeh ta hay" while pronouncing it "yettahey." Neither will get even a nod of recognition on the reservation.

Further complicating the situation is the fact that the Navajos themselves pronounce and spell it differently. A brochure published by Navajo Tourism says it's "ya a' teeh." (That's not really the correct spelling because there are diacritical marks over the first *a* and the two *e*'s.) Another form is "yaa' teeh." One more is "ya'at' eeh." All, of course, with those marks over the vowels.

Yet-tah-hey:

A Navajo greeting becoming increasingly popular with Anglos who want others to think they're bilingual.

Extended research into the matter has led to the conclusion that when in Navajo land, non-Navajos should stick with the basics and just say "hello" or "goodbye" instead of making fools of themselves trying to pronounce something they don't know how to spell, and vice versa.

you know you're in
arizona when ...
... an old prison still causes shudders

The Yuma Territorial Prison is not a pretty place, but thousands go there anyway. Some bad people were incarcerated in the prison, an infamous part of the Old West. But it wasn't as bad as depicted in either the movies or the wild-and-wooly tales people tell about it.

In the stories, those who were incarcerated there are often described as desperate men and women with no redeeming qualities. But in truth, many of them wouldn't even go to prison today for some of the crimes they committed more than a century ago.

The prison opened in 1876 when seven inmates were locked into the cells they helped build. Over the next thirty-three years, a total of 3,069 prisoners (29 of them women) were confined inside the walls for crimes ranging from murder to polygamy to seduction. Most didn't serve their full sentences, as paroles and pardons were relatively easy to come by.

Yuma Territorial wasn't a bad place to repay and repent. The prisoners could learn a trade like blacksmithing, shoemaking, electrical work, or carpentry. They had access to a well-stocked library, running water, flush toilets, and forced-air ventilation, things the townspeople of Yuma didn't even have. Perhaps understandably, this produced some animosity, and the prison became known as "the Country Club on the Colorado River." The *Arizona Sentinel* grumbled: "One can go any day to the prison and see convicts singing and skylarking, joking and all-in-all having a grand old time at the expense of the taxpayer. It is well-known here that the prison on the hill is more a place of recreation and amusement than servitude."

The prison closed in 1909. It later served as a high school (the Yuma High School athletic teams are still nicknamed the Criminals), movie set, office space, and a VFW post before being converted into a museum in the 1940s. Now it's a tourist attraction where people can examine the cells and be glad they've been good.

Yuma Prison:

Now a tourist attraction, this prison was once considered the toughest incarceration hole in the Territory.

index

THE INSIDER'S SOURCE

With more than 120 Southwest-related titles, we have the area covered. Whether you're looking for the path less traveled, a favorite place to eat, family-friendly fun, a breathtaking hike, or enchanting local attractions, our pages are filled with ideas to get you from one state to the next.

For a complete listing of all our titles, please visit our Web site at www.GlobePequot.com. The Globe Pequot Press is the largest publisher of local travel books in the United States and is a leading source for outdoor recreation guides.

FOR BOOKS TO THE SOUTHWEST

INSIDERS' GUIDE®

FALCON GUIDE®

Available wherever books are sold.
Orders can also be placed on the Web at www.GlobePequot.com,
by phone from 8:00 A.M. to 5:00 P.M. at 1-800-243-0495,
or by fax at 1-800-820-2329.